MW00426230

The
Psych
101
Series

James C. Kaufman, PhD, Series Editor
Department of Educational Psychology
University of Connecticut

Jonathan A. Plucker, PhD, is an endowed professor of education at the Neag School of Education at the University of Connecticut, teaching in the educational psychology and the educational leadership and policy programs. He previously served as a professor of educational psychology and cognitive science at Indiana University. He is past chair of the Research and Evaluation Division of the National Association for Gifted Children and past president of the Society for the Psychology of Aesthetics, Creativity, and the Arts, American Psychological Association (APA) Division 10. He has received numerous awards for his research, including the Early Scholar and Paul Torrance awards from the National Association for Gifted Children, the Berlyne and Arnheim awards from APA Division 10, and two awards from the Mensa Education and Research Foundation for Excellence in Research. He is an elected fellow of the APA and the American Association for the Advancement of Science. Dr. Plucker frequently teaches and lectures around the world on topics related to intelligence, creativity, and talent, and he has recently served as a visiting scholar at universities in China, Australia, and the United States. He is the creator of the website Human Intelligence: Historical Influences, Current Controversies, Teaching Resources (www.intelltheory.com).

Amber Esping, PhD, is an assistant professor of educational psychology at Texas Christian University in Fort Worth. Her research focuses on the history of intelligence theory and testing and the application of existential psychology to academic contexts and qualitative inquiry. She and Jonathan Plucker were co-recipients of the Instructional Resource Award from the Society for the Teaching of Psychology for their work with the website Human Intelligence: Historical Influences, Current Controversies, Teaching Resources, for which she has served as co-director since 2005.

Intelligence
101

Jonathan A. Plucker, PhD
Amber Esping, PhD

SPRINGER PUBLISHING COMPANY
NEW YORK

Springer Publishing Company, LLC
11 West 42nd Street
New York, NY 10036
www.springerpub.com

Acquisitions Editor: Nancy S. Hale
Composition: Amnet

ISBN: 978-0-8261-1125-8
e-book ISBN: 978-0-8261-1126-5

13 14 15 16 / 5 4 3 2 1

The author and the publisher of this Work have made every effort to use sources believed
to be reliable to provide information that is accurate and compatible with the standards
generally accepted at the time of publication. The author and publisher shall not be
liable for any special, consequential, or exemplary damages resulting, in whole or in
part, from the readers' use of, or reliance on, the information contained in this book.
The publisher has no responsibility for the persistence or accuracy of URLs for external
or third-party Internet websites referred to in this publication and does not guarantee
that any content on such websites is, or will remain, accurate or appropriate.

Library of Congress Cataloging-in-Publication Data

Plucker, Jonathan A., 1969–
  Intelligence 101 / Jonathan Plucker, PhD, Amber Esping, PhD.
     pages cm.—(Psych 101)
  Includes bibliographical references and index.
  ISBN 978-0-8261-1125-8 (print edition : alk. paper)—ISBN 978-0-8261-1126-5
(e-book) 1. Intellect. I. Esping, Amber. II. Title.
  BF431.P5698 2014
  153.9—dc23

                                                                    2013029360

Printed in the United States of America by Gasch Printing.

To Kathleen, Paige, and Jack, who make it all worthwhile.

—J. A. P.

For Thomas and Dylan. Ecclesiastes 4:12.

—A. E.

Contents

CONTENTS

Preface

As researchers who study both creativity and intelligence, over time we have encountered very different reactions to this work from colleagues. On one hand, we get lots of comments like "Why are you bothering with intelligence when that creativity stuff is so interesting?" On the other hand, we also get comments along the lines of "Why are you not focusing more time on your intelligence work—you know, the scientific stuff?"

These comments reflect a paradox about the study of human intelligence that has been both a blessing and a curse: People generally don't think the topic is all that interesting, at least compared with other psychological constructs, but they also consider it to be a serious scientific enterprise. That sounds like the definition of "boring science" to us!

Admittedly, when we first encountered the topic in graduate school, our initial reaction was not "Wow, this will be super exciting!" But as we read a few good overviews of the topic (many of which are listed later in this book), we came to realize that intelligence is *not* boring. On the contrary, it is often outrageously controversial. As we learned about the interesting theories and research, then about scandals, sex, football, and social Darwinism, and then about more accusations of fraud and underhandedness than can be imagined, we decided, "Sign us up!"

After all, a well-known figure in the history of intelligence was the first football coach at the University of Southern California. One of the most famous psychologists who ever lived may have fabricated huge amounts of data on intelligence, perhaps even the majority of his work—or maybe he didn't. In the first half of the 20th century the Nazis translated a popular American book about intelligence into German and used it to justify their agenda. Researchers now widely consider one of the most popular late-20th-century books on intelligence to be full of mistakes and mischaracterizations, yet it remains popular and is still used as a textbook in college classes. In many ways, the study of intelligence mirrors the history of psychology and the social sciences in general, and it has often been intertwined with major developments and debates in the wider society. For example, intelligence testing played a key role in World War I, debates over immigration policy have often focused on intelligence, and the publication of *The Bell Curve* in the early 1990s led to tremendous controversy and debates across our society.

As we move further into the 21st century, advances in genetics research and neuroimaging technology will undoubtedly raise new questions and provide fodder for fresh controversies. Human intelligence will continue to fascinate and agitate psychologists, educators, students, and the general public. We hope that this book will help draw you in so that you can become part of these conversations.

Acknowledgments

Our perspectives on intelligence have been influenced by a number of scholars over the past few decades. In particular, the writings of Raymond Fancher were the first author's entrée into intelligence theory and research, and Fancher's engaging approach to the history of the study of human intelligence was a major influence on how we approached this project. We also appreciate the time and contributions of several other eminent scholars on a range of issues over the years, including Camilla Benbow, Carolyn Callahan, Hudson Cattell (grandson of James McKeen Cattell), Jack Cummings, J. P. Das, Douglas Detterman, Carol Dweck, Donna Ford, Howard Gardner, Alan and Nadeen Kaufman, David Lubinski, Charles Murray, Jack Naglieri, Joe Renzulli, Dean Keith Simonton, and Bob Sternberg. Their willingness to provide input and constructive criticism to our work, debate us from time to time, and provide support strongly influenced our continued desire to study intelligence and ultimately made this book possible.

In addition, we consider ourselves fortunate to have corresponded with some of the major figures in human intelligence research before they passed away. Raymond Cattell, John Carroll, and John Horn provided their valuable, unique perspectives near the end of their lives. Professor Carroll and Professor Horn were especially generous with their time, and we consider ourselves fortunate to have extensive written correspondence from Professor Carroll and lengthy video with Professor Horn in which they discussed their views of intelligence and enthusiastically answered our questions about their work.

Much of this material developed as we taught aspects of human intelligence to our students at several different universities. The students' input is reflected in this volume both in the content we chose to highlight and in the way that content was presented. We are grateful for the students' input.

Last but not least, we acknowledge our editors, Nancy S. Hale at Springer Publishing Company and James Kaufman, the series editor. They showed superhuman levels of patience with this project as it evolved, circled around itself, and took on a life of its own. We hope the finished product is worthy of the input of all of the individuals listed above.

Intelligence 101

Why Intelligence Rocks

Perhaps no concept in psychology has been investigated as comprehensively—or controversially—as human intelligence. This attention is long-standing: Theories of intelligence predate the formal establishment of psychology as a science by millennia. Although perhaps more commonly associated with philosophy, the ideas of Aristotle, Socrates, and Plato all contribute to the foundation of our understanding of the nature of human intelligence. Their ideas on topics as diverse as the origin of ability, the mind–body relationship, and general inquiry methods continued to inspire thinkers centuries later and influenced those who shaped modern psychology and intelligence theory. Philosophers, psychologists, and educators have spent much of the past 2 centuries building on the foundations of the ancient thinkers, and a variety of theories and conceptions of intelligence have resulted.

CHAPTER 1

Intelligence has also been among the most controversial constructs in all of the social sciences. After all, the answer to a question as fundamental as "What is intelligence?" has tremendous implications for how one views people. Is intelligence a "thing" or a collection of things? Are racial and socioeconomic differences in measured intelligence evidence of nature or nurture effects? Is intelligence organic or immutable? How different people answer these questions tells us a lot about how they view others, how they approach learning and problem solving, and how they view themselves. The purpose of this book is to provide a widely accessible introduction to the topic of human intelligence, with a careful presentation of the wide range of potential answers to these questions.

ORGANIZATION OF THE BOOK

In the following chapters, we present a number of important topics. The difficulty we faced in putting this material together is that there is simply so much to discuss. A truly exhaustive approach would fill thousands of pages, which isn't appropriate for a general introduction such as this. In addition, it would be dreadfully boring, and we promised ourselves we would not write that type of book! We have selected material that we personally find to be the most interesting, but keep in mind that this book is not intended to cover every important topic and relate every interesting story.[1]

We start our adventures in this chapter with an overview of our approach to the topic, and in Chapter 2 we review some definitions of intelligence. Then we explore the origins of the psychological study of intelligence by examining the fascinating legacy of Francis Galton's work. In Chapter 4 we examine the impact of education and other attempts to develop intelligence by reviewing the work of Henry Goddard and looking at his complicated reputation.

The next section of the book focuses more closely on recent developments in research regarding intelligence. We first delve into the debate over whether intelligence is unitary or multifaceted; this chapter includes a brief overview of recent research on how people's beliefs about intelligence impact their behaviors, a body of research that has significant implications for education. Then we examine issues of nature and nurture in the development of intelligence, primarily by presenting the curious phenomenon of the Flynn effect. This section concludes with an examination of the relationships between intelligence and related constructs such as creativity and giftedness.

We close the book with some thoughts about where we believe the study of intelligence will be heading over the next few decades. A list of recommended resources is included at the end of the book. One subject this book does not focus on is testing, at least not the mechanics and broader theoretical issues related to assessment. Those topics have been covered in great depth (and handled quite well) elsewhere, most notably in the work of A. Kaufman (2009).

WHY A HISTORICAL APPROACH?

You'll find that each chapter is approached largely from a historical perspective. This is the perspective from which we first approached this topic. Intelligence has been covered from other perspectives in several books over the past 20 years, many of which are outstanding and are listed in the Recommended Resources section. But we find the historical approach to be quite interesting and straightforward, and a perspective that is not terribly common in books on intelligence.

For that reason, we designed our website—Human Intelligence: Historical Influences, Current Controversies, and Teaching Resources (www.intelltheory.com)—with a strong historical theme when we put it together in the 1990s. The site was built on the framework of a complex diagram representing all the relationships and intellectual influences of the many people who have studied intelligence. We chose not to reproduce that diagram in this book, in part because it provides too much detail for our purposes here, but also because the graphic simply works better in a virtual environment.

As we began populating the site with material, the chart was overlaid with six distinct time periods, which were intended as guides and not rigid barriers. For example, several scholars worked across two or more time periods, such as John Carroll; his career falls predominantly within the Contemporary Explorations period, yet he is most often remembered for his seminal work in 1993, during the Current Efforts time period. As we view them, the six "ages of intelligence" are the following.

Historical Foundations

The nature of the human intellect has fascinated scholars for centuries. Indeed, the origins of modern intelligence theory can be traced at least as far back as Plato and Aristotle, centuries before the start of the Common Era. For example, Aristotle foreshadowed debates about whether intelligence is one thing or many things when he distinguished between intellectual excellence and moral excellence, and with his division of mental activities into three categories: understanding, action, and production (Tigner & Tigner, 2000). And Plato, Aristotle's teacher, entered the nature versus nurture debate when he asked, "Can you tell me, Socrates, whether excellence can be taught? Or can it not be taught, but acquired through practice? Or can it neither be acquired through practice nor learned, but is something which men possess by nature or in some other way?" (Plato, trans. 1985, p. 35). This largely, but not exclusively, philosophical approach to the study of human intellectual capacity continued for roughly 2 millennia, involving the work of Hume, Kant, Adam Smith, and many others.

Modern Foundations

During the 1800s, psychology began to emerge as a discipline separate from philosophy, mathematics, and biology. In addition, significant advances were made in the study of intelligence. Building on the strong historical foundations mentioned above, philosophers and psychologists made significant contributions to our understanding of intelligence. Two major figures from this time, holding very different views of the development of intelligence, are the psychologist Francis Galton, building on the work of his half-cousin Charles Darwin, and the philosopher John Stuart Mill.

The Great Schools

The late 1800s saw the growth of psychology as a distinct scientific field, and the formation of major schools of psychology in Europe and, later, in the United States hastened the development of the psychological sciences. The study of intelligence as a major focal point of psychology proceeded along a similar path. In particular, the influences of Wilhelm Wundt, James McKeen Cattell, G. S. Hall, and Hermann Ebbinghaus were considerable. The most notable development of this time period is the refinement of the work of Galton and other earlier researchers, particularly James McKeen Cattell, in Germany, England, and later the United States.

The Great Schools' Influence

As the students of the Great Schools began to study intelligence (and form their own programs throughout the developed world), theoretical and empirical investigations of intelligence blossomed. Within this context, a great deal of seminal work on intelligence was conducted, including the work of Alfred Binet, Lewis Terman, Charles Spearman, Henry Goddard, Robert Mearns Yerkes, and the U.S. Army testing team during the First World War.

Contemporary Explorations

The influence of the Great Schools and the Army testing program was still being felt several years later. The period between the end of the First World War and the late 1960s is best known for the development of intelligence testing, a time when the combination of modern statistics and advances in testing helped to make standardized testing of intelligence and achievement a way of life in most Western countries. In addition, several important theoretical and empirical advances were made by L. L. Thurstone, David Wechsler, J. P. Guilford, John Horn, and Raymond Cattell, among others. A defining characteristic of these research programs is the reliance on psychometrics and statistical methodology for studying intelligence. This stands in contrast to later efforts, which are more diverse in their theoretical and methodological approaches. Although g-centric theories dominated this period, multiple intelligence theories begin to appear in the work of Thurstone and Guilford.

Current Efforts

Over the past 30 to 40 years, several important contributions have been made in the development of intelligence theory. Current trends in intelligence theory and research involve the formation of more complex multiple intelligence theories and a de-emphasis on the use of standardized testing to measure intelligence. The emergence of reliable genetic and neurological research methodologies is creating a new area of study in which environmental, biological, and psychological facets of intelligence are studied simultaneously. Much of the 1980s was marked by the analysis of Gardner's and Sternberg's work with multiple intelligences, and over the past 2 decades a diverse set of theoretical approaches have been proposed, studied, and refined, including PASS theory and emotional intelligence. A flurry of controversy in the mid-1990s provided evidence that reports of the death of psychometric, unitary approaches to intelligences have been greatly exaggerated.

Although the identification of these time periods has met its stated objective (i.e., facilitating an understanding of dominant themes in the study of intelligence), you should be aware that a seventh period is emerging, and we explore this work and its implications in the book's final chapter. Recent technological advances have encouraged explorations into the relationship between brain function and specific types of cognitive functioning. We anticipate that the Current Efforts period will eventually be relabeled Tensions and Reconceptualizations, with the new, seventh era to be referred to as Current Efforts, having a heavy neurological emphasis. The future of intelligence research looks exciting, and we can't wait to see what will happen next!

TAKEAWAYS

- Perhaps no idea or concept in psychology has been investigated as comprehensively—or controversially—as human intelligence.

- The development of the study of intelligence parallels the development of psychology as a scientific field.
- Taking a historical approach to this topic can help us understand many developments in the field that, taken out of their temporal context, appear disconnected and often unfathomable.

NOTE

1. For example, we find Guilford's work with his Structure of Intellect (SOI) model to be fascinating, as it represents a very different approach to theories of intelligence. Guilford studied and modified his model throughout his career, right up until he passed away, so the SOI model also serves as a compelling case study about how theories are developed, tested, and revised over time. But the SOI model, in our estimation, is not a major player among intelligence theories these days, and other theories have been more influential over the past century. If we ever write *Intelligence 201*, Guilford is sure to be prominently featured in it. But for now, his work (and the work of other interesting people such as Godfrey Thomson) is excluded so that we can focus on the most compelling work and stories. Similarly, we originally intended to devote an entire chapter to the major longitudinal studies that involve intelligence, but that would send us too far into the weeds. Rather, we refer to these studies throughout the book and encourage interested readers to consult the excellent summaries of these studies that are already available (e.g., Deary, Whalley, & Starr, 2009; Lubinski & Benbow, 2006; Schaie, 2005; Shurkin, 1992).

Defining Intelligence

WHAT IS A CONSTRUCT?

Intelligence does not exist—on this planet or anywhere else.

This strange statement is not an attempt to be clever. It is a fundamental truth about human intelligence that you must understand before you can appreciate the challenges faced by the psychologists who study this sometimes slippery and elusive subject.

Consider this scenario. You are an alien from another planet who has landed on Earth as part of a group looking for intelligent life. You are not looking for intelligence itself, because intelligence is not a physical thing that can be seen or measured in the way physicists see and measure matter. Rather, intelligence is a hypothesized quality whose ontology, etiology, and scale must be inferred through indirect means. For instance, intelligence is assumed to originate in the brain, but it is not made of matter (as a dedicated intelligence organ is); nor is it a discrete, incarnate force emanating from the brain that can be measured directly with sophisticated equipment. There is absolutely nothing physical that you can put a ruler next to and say, "This is how much intelligence is here" (e.g., Thorndike, 1997). To paraphrase Gertrude Stein, "There isn't any there there."

This condition isn't unique to intelligence; there are many psychological constructs that we deal with every day. Happiness is a good example: You can't buy some happiness (although many have tried!), there is no store that has boxes of happiness on the shelf, and you can't give a friend a box of happiness on his or her birthday.

Yet, clearly, we all know what happiness is, right? From a scientific point of view, there is a collection of behaviors, emotions, and attitudes that can be observed that describe this "thing" we call happiness. But that's actually the root of the problem: These constructs need to be defined, and one person's definition may be very different from another's. This "definition of constructs" issue can be observed in many areas of psychology, including creativity and giftedness, which we'll discuss in a later chapter.

Since intelligence is not a thing that can be directly seen or felt, you and your alien companions would have to be content with looking for *signs* or *evidence* of earthly intelligence, based on the kinds of observable behaviors you believe intelligence leads to. For instance, you might decide to look for evidence of technology, sophisticated social structures, artistic and philosophical accomplishments, or the ability to master one's environment. The evidence you find would lead you to make conclusions about the presence or absence of intelligence on this planet, and to make some preliminary judgments about the nature and magnitude of that intelligence. However, these judgments may or may not gel with the conclusions drawn by another alien group visiting this planet, because they might be looking for different evidence than you are. For instance, they may believe that the ability to live in harmony with one's environment—rather than master it—is evidence of intelligence.

You and the other group of alien visitors could probably each come up with reasonable and persuasive arguments to justify your divergent positions. This is one reason why the field of intelligence theory has always generated controversy and discord. Like many important phenomena of interest in the social and behavioral sciences, human intelligence is a psychological construct (or, more precisely, a set of opposing and complementary psychological constructs developed by many influential researchers at different points in history). A construct is a defensible cluster of quantifiable, isolable qualities and attributes that, taken together, form a measurable representation of a multifaceted, hypothesized abstraction (Thorndike, 1997). In the alien visitor metaphor, we have two constructs of intelligence: the specific cluster of signs and evidence of intelligence your group decided to look for, and the slightly different cluster of signs and evidence the other group is looking for.

The alien visitor metaphor oversimplifies the issues, however. In real life, creating a construct for intelligence is always a highly technical endeavor, grounded in measurement theory (Stevens, 1946) and the science of psychometrics (literally, "measuring the mind"). But the broader takeaway here is that definitions are critically important when one is dealing with psychological constructs, and intelligence is no exception. If two researchers define intelligence in widely different ways, their studies may produce conflicting results. There is often much hair pulling and gnashing of teeth when research studies contradict each other, but we are always surprised when researchers skip the logical first step for comparing results: Check the underlying definitions to see what each research team was actually studying.

PERSONAL DEFINITIONS OF INTELLIGENCE

Personal definitions of intelligence are not the same as constructs of intelligence. Psychological constructs are highly technical, painstakingly crafted, and subjected to rigorous theoretical examination and empirical testing (see Kaufman, 2009; Thorndike, 1997). Personal definitions of intelligence are much looser, providing a sort of shorthand, CliffsNotes version of the various theorists' intelligence constructs. These definitions can be very useful because they are straightforward statements that provide easy access to each theorist's beliefs about intelligence. Moreover, these statements often contain clues as to where the theorist believes intelligence comes from. This is something that may be absent from constructs, and as you will see in subsequent chapters, this has been, and remains, a major area of controversy.

Another reason personal definitions of intelligence are useful is that they sometimes contain important contextual clues, including a general sense of the evolution of the field of intelligence theory over time, a window into a priori values and assumptions derived from the zeitgeist in which the theorists were living, and some insight into the broader worldviews that were influencing, and being influenced by, a particular theorist's work (see Kuhn, 1962/2012). It is also sometimes possible to see the imprint of a theorist's personal history on the way he or she defines human intellectual ability. Consider Sir Francis Galton, for example. As a eugenicist, he was specifically interested in the identification and proliferation of individuals at the high end of the human intellectual spectrum.[1] He adopted the term *genius* to refer to these people in his writings.[1] He explained his use of the term *genius* as indicating

> an ability that was exceptionally high, and at the same time inborn. It was intended to be used in the senses ascribed to the word in Johnson's Dictionary, viz. "Mental power or faculties. Disposition

of nature by which any one is qualified to some peculiar employ-ment. Nature; disposition." A person who is a genius is denned as—A man endowed with superior faculties. . . . [Genius] is freely used as an equivalent for natural ability. (Galton, 1892, pp. vii–ix)

Strictly speaking, Galton was not interested in everyone's intelligence, just that of geniuses. This by itself is interesting and illustrative; Galton's focus on geniuses is in some ways representative of his zeitgeist, which was heavily influenced by the writings of his cousin Charles Darwin. The significance of heredity was nearly dripping from the air Galton breathed. Consider the following review of Galton's most famous work (and arguably the first psychological study of intelligence), *Hereditary Genius*:

Mr. Galton hastens to admit that his views . . . are "in contradic-tion to general opinion." We believe, on the other hand, that the crudely formed opinions of the general public are quite as often to be found on Mr. Galton's side as on the opposite. . . . In this case . . . popular prejudice is unequivocally supported by scien-tific investigation. . . . A man like Newton must have had parents of rare mental capacity, even though they have done nothing by which to be remembered in history: the son of ordinary parents could no more have discovered the law of gravitation than the offspring of a pair of cart-horses could win the Derby. (*Atlantic Monthly*, 1870, p. 753)

Galton's personal history also may have influenced his defi-nition of genius. By almost any objective measure, Galton was an extraordinarily successful man; indeed, posterity has deemed him a genius (e.g., Simonton, 2009). However, his autobio-graphical writings suggest that despite his efforts to better him-self, he never quite lived up to his own academic expectations. It is not surprising, then, given his personal history and society's attitudes toward heredity, that Galton concluded that the devel-opment of genius must be understood in terms of hereditary processes (see Fancher, 1985; Simonton, 2009). As we will see in a later chapter, this was not the inevitable interpretation of his empirical findings. Although he contributed many things of significance to the work of intelligence researchers who came after him, there can be little doubt that a priori assumptions prevented him from acknowledging in his studies the importance of mechanisms other than heredity that were at work. Definitions clearly matter, and they can tell us a lot about the people who created them.

SOME EXAMPLES OF DEFINITIONS

It is perhaps an exaggeration to invoke Gibson's law here ("for every PhD there is an equal and opposite PhD")[2] because there are recognized schools of thought regarding human intelligence, and it would be unfair to represent the field as filled with philosophical mavericks who never find consensus. However, it should be clear by now that there are many ways to conceptualize human intellectual ability. For instance, each of the following three definitions of human intelligence was proven in its time to be useful, influential, and empirically or theoretically justifiable:

> It seems to us that in intelligence there is a fundamental faculty, the alteration or the lack of which, is of the utmost importance for practical life. This faculty is judgment, otherwise called good sense, practical sense, initiative, the faculty of adapting one's self to circumstances. A person may be a moron or an imbecile if he is lacking in judgment; but with good judgment he can never be either. Indeed the rest of the intellectual faculties seem of little importance in comparison with judgment. (Binet & Simon, 1916/1973, pp. 42–43).

A working definition of intelligence . . . is that it is the *g* factor of an indefinitely large and varied battery of mental tests. . . . We are forced to infer that *g* [the symbol for the hypothetical construct of "general intelligence," a kind of generalized intellectual force or power presumed to underlie all mental activities to one degree or another] is of considerable importance in "real life" by the fact that *g* constitutes the largest component of total variance in all standard tests of intelligence or IQ, and the very same *g* is by far the largest component of variance in scholastic achievement. (Jensen, 1979, pp. 249–250)

I define [intelligence] as your skill in achieving whatever it is you want to attain in your life within your sociocultural context by capitalizing on your strengths and compensating for, or correcting, your weaknesses. (R. J. Sternberg, personal communication, July 29, 2004)

We see here intelligence defined variously as the capacity for exercising judgment (Binet, 1916), mathematical relationships among test scores (Jensen, 1979), and the ability to capitalize on strengths and to compensate or correct for weaknesses within a particular context (Sternberg, personal communication, July 29, 2004). This small sample illustrates the range of positions taken in the literature on human intelligence, a range that also offers a sense of the historical development of how scholars have viewed intelligence.

We close this chapter with two tables presenting definitions of intelligence provided by several prominent historical and living intelligence theorists (Tables 2.1 and 2.2). They are by no means comprehensive, but they provide a sense of the scope of the field. Due to space limitations, we can't possibly discuss the work of all of these theorists. However, we include these tables to convince you that human intelligence is a fascinating and complex subject, and to provide a foreshadowing of many of the essential issues that will be discussed in subsequent chapters.

Francis Galton (1822–1911), British psychologist	"[Genius is] an ability that was exceptionally high, and at the same time inborn. It was intended to be used in the senses ascribed to the word in Johnson's Dictionary, viz. 'Mental power or faculties. Disposition of nature by which any one is qualified to some peculiar employment. Nature; disposition.' A person who is a genius is denned as—A man endowed with superior faculties. . . . [Genius] is freely used as an equivalent for natural ability." (Galton, 1892, pp. vii–ix)
Alfred Binet (1857–1911) and Theodore Simon (1873–1961), French psychologists	"It seems to us that in intelligence there is a fundamental faculty, the alteration or the lack of which, is of the utmost importance for practical life. This faculty is judgment, otherwise called good sense, practical sense, initiative, the faculty of adapting one's self to circumstances. A person may be a moron or an imbecile [terms no longer in professional use today, but previously used to designate the most severe degrees of mental disability; to be described more fully later] if he is lacking in judgment; but with good judgment he can never be either. Indeed the rest of the intellectual faculties seem of little importance in comparison with judgment." (Binet & Simon, 1916/1973, pp. 42–43)
Charles Spearman (1863–1945), British psychologist	"As regards the delicate matter of estimating 'Intelligence,' the guiding principle has been not to make any *a priori* assumptions as to what kind of mental activity may be thus termed with greatest propriety. Provisionally, at any rate, the aim was empirically to examine all the various abilities having any *prima facie* claims to such title, ascertaining their relations to one another and to other functions." (Spearman, 1904, pp. 249–250)
Henry Herbert Goddard (1866–1957), American psychologist	"[O]ur thesis is that the chief determiner of human conduct is a unitary mental process which we call intelligence: that this process is conditioned by a nervous mechanism which is inborn: that the degree of efficiency to be attained by that nervous mechanism and the consequent grade of intelligence or mental level for each individual is determined by the kind of chromosomes that come together with the union of the germ cells: that it is but little affected by any later influences except such serious accidents as may destroy part of the mechanism." (Goddard, 1920, p. 1)

Robert Mearns Yerkes (1876–1956), American psychologist	"The term intelligence designates a complexly interrelated assemblage of functions, no one of which is completely or accurately known in man." (Yerkes, 1929, p. 524)
Lewis Terman (1877–1956), American psychologist	"Intelligence is the ability to think in terms of abstract ideas." (Terman, 1921, p. 129)
Cyril Burt (1883–1971), British psychologist	"[Intelligence] denotes, first of all, a quality that is intellectual and not emotional or moral: in measuring it we try to rule out the effects of the child's zeal, interest, industry, and the like. Secondly, it denotes a general capacity, a capacity that enters into everything the child says or does or thinks; any want of 'intelligence' will therefore be revealed to some degree in almost all that he attempts; a weakness in some limited or specialized ability—for example, in the ability to speak or to read, to learn or to calculate—is of itself by no means a sign of defective intelligence. Thirdly, intelligence is by definition an innate capacity: hence a lack of it is not necessarily proved by a lack of educational knowledge or skill." (Burt, 1957, pp. 64–65)
David Wechsler (1896–1981), American psychologist	"Intelligence is the aggregate or global capacity of the individual to act purposefully, to think rationally and to deal effectively with his environment." (Wechsler, 1944, p. 3)
Hans Eysenck (1916–1997), German-born British psychologist	"If we can derive a model of the intellect . . . from the existing literature, it may be suggested that a combination of Spearman's *g*, Thurstone's primary abilities (grouped under mental processes and test material), and the break-down of the IQ into speed, persistence and error-checking, may be the best available at the moment." (Eysenck, 1979, p. 193)

(continued)

TABLE 2.1 PERSONAL DEFINITIONS OF INTELLIGENCE FROM PROMINENT HISTORICAL THEORISTS (continued)

Arthur Jensen (1923–2012), American psychologist	"A working definition of intelligence . . . is that it is the g factor of an indefinitely large and varied battery of mental tests. . . . We are forced to infer that g is of considerable importance in 'real life' by the fact that g constitutes the largest component of total variance in all standard tests of intelligence or IQ, and the very same g is by far the largest component of variance in scholastic achievement." (Jensen, 1979, pp. 249–250)
John L. Horn (1928–2006), American psychologist	"Intellectual abilities are organized at a general level into two general intelligences, viz., fluid intelligence and crystallized intelligence. These represent the operation of . . . independent . . . influences in development. On the one hand there are those influences which directly affect the physiological structure upon which intellectual processes must be constructed—influences operating through the agencies of heredity and injury: these are most accurately reflected in measures of fluid intelligence. And on the other hand there are those influences which affect physiological structure only indirectly through agencies of learnings and acculturations, etc.: crystallized intelligence is the most direct resultant of individual differences in these influences." (Horn & Cattell, 1967, p. 109)
John B. Carroll (1916–2003), American psychologist	"The three-stratum theory of cognitive abilities is an expansion and extension of previous theories. It specifies what kinds of individual differences in cognitive abilities exist and how those kinds of individual differences are related to one another. It proposes that there are a fairly large number of distinct individual differences in cognitive ability, and that the relationships among them can be derived by classifying them into three different strata: stratum I, 'narrow' abilities; stratum II, 'broad' abilities; and stratum III, consisting of a single 'general' ability." (Carroll, 1997, p. 122)

Jagannath Prasad (J. P.) Das (b. 1931), Canadian psychologist	"Intelligence is the sum total of all cognitive processes. It entails planning, coding of information and attention, as well as arousal." (Das, personal communication, November 24, 2004)
Douglas K. Detterman (b. 1942), American psychologist	"Intelligence is not an easy thing to define, and in fact it's even more difficult because any words associated with intellectual ability or intelligence become corrupted with common use. Words like *moron, idiot,* and *imbecile* [terms no longer in professional use today, but previously used to designate the most severe degrees of mental disability] all started off as scientific terms, but they've been corrupted by common use. . . . So I think a better approach is to define things like general intelligence, or *g,* where we have a mathematical definition, and where we can attempt to get a scientific explanation of the construct. . . . That is, we can define *g*—general intelligence—in terms of correlations among mental tests, and then attempt to explain that *g* using theory and empirical tests. . . . That's essentially what I've done, is to try to understand *g,* which I think is a major component of mental ability." (Detterman, personal communication, August 23, 2002)
Howard Gardner (b. 1943), American psychologist	"An intelligence is the ability to solve problems, or to create products, that are valued within one or more cultural settings." (Gardner, 1983, p. x)
Alan S. Kaufman (b. 1944), American psychologist	"What used to be was Wechsler saying, 'There's *g,* or maybe there are these two main ways we can express *g*—verbally and nonverbally.' I think now it makes more sense to think that we should be measuring a wider array of abilities, and whether that number is 4 or 5 or 6 or 7, from Wechsler's perspective, if you're measuring something called intelligence it should still be complex. And if you try to make abilities very narrow to fit a theory very precisely

(continued)

19

	then I think you are losing the essence of what we as intelligent people can do, which is think in very complex ways. So we have not strived for factor purity. We used factor analysis results to support our scales, and they do. But we deliberately make our scales impure to match what we believe is inside people—a complex way of approaching the world." (Kaufman, personal communication, July 31, 2004)
Dean Keith Simonton (b. 1948), American psychologist	"My view of intelligence is basically a Darwinian one. It's based on sort of the old Functionalist notion that goes way back to Francis Galton, that says that there are a certain set of cognitive capacities that enable an individual to adapt and thrive in any given environment they find themselves in, and those cognitive capacities include things like memory and retrieval, and problem solving and so forth. There's a cluster of cognitive abilities that lead to successful adaptation to a wide range of environments." (Simonton, personal communication, July 5, 2003)
Robert Sternberg (b. 1949), American psychologist	"I define [intelligence] as your skill in achieving whatever it is you want to attain in your life within your sociocultural context by capitalizing on your strengths and compensating for, or correcting, your weaknesses." (Sternberg, personal communication, July 29, 2004)
Camilla Benbow (b. 1956) and David Lubinski (b. 1953), American psychologists	"[Intelligence] has a general factor at its summit . . . that accounts for approximately half of the variation in individual differences in human intellectual functions, and people name that function differently. Some talk about it as an intellectual sophistication function, general intelligence, *g*. They're pretty much the same thing. And then there are specific abilities—specific factors—that are more molecular, that have to do with spatial reasoning, verbal reasoning, quantitative reasoning. And they go down to more molecular strands after that." (David Lubinski, speaking in a joint interview with Camilla Benbow, July 23, 2003)

TAKEAWAYS

- Intelligence is a psychological construct, and this makes its definition very important.
- Famous researchers and theorists have defined intelligence many different ways, which has implications for our understanding of their work.

NOTES

1. Other eugenicist researchers focused their attention on the opposite end of the intelligence spectrum, attempting to understand the causes and consequences of low intelligence, and thereby to prevent individuals with limited intelligence from passing along their hereditary endowments to subsequent generations. You will read about one such eugenicist, Henry Herbert Goddard, in a later chapter.
2. This "law" pays homage to Newton's third law ("for every action there is an equal and opposite reaction"). It was first used in public relations, and originally referred to contradicting expert testimonies in court cases (Proctor, 2001).

Origins of the Study of Intelligence: The Case of Galton

(*continued*)
a child with another genius, you are helping to increase the number of geniuses in the world. And that's good for everyone! There is no fee for this service.*

---

*Nongeniuses are encouraged to abstain from having children. If you are an ordinary person, please support this service by making a charitable donation to help defray the costs incurred by the creation of large families of geniuses. For information about birth control or to donate money to support local genius families, go to www.intelltheory .com/geniusmatch.

Obviously, we concocted this advertisement, and GeniusMatch. com does not really exist. This dating service is our tongue-in-cheek take on a real proposition advocated by the British psychologist Sir Francis Galton (1822–1911) in several publications in the mid-1800s. You might be surprised to learn that it was Galton who came up with the concept of the intelligence test as a way to identify potential geniuses while they were still young enough to marry and procreate. The "Golden Book of Natural Nobility" and the radical redefinition of charity presented in our satire were also suggested by Galton. Fortunately for posterity, these suggestions didn't take, but his concept of intelligence testing did. In addition to intelligence testing, Galton had many other fruitful ideas for which contemporary intelligence theory and testing owe him a large debt of gratitude. This chapter will explore some of his many contributions.

GALTON'S CONTRIBUTIONS TO INTELLIGENCE THEORY AND TESTING

Sir Francis Galton was a polymath who achieved eminence in many areas before turning his attention toward psychology. He distinguished himself first as an African explorer, travel writer, and Fellow of the Royal Geographic Society (e.g., Galton, 1851, 1853a, 1853b). He created the first modern weather map and established the meteorological theory of alternating high- and low-pressure systems (Galton, 1861a). These endeavors laid the foundation for Galton's most important work, but he was of middle age before he made significant contributions to the development of intelligence theory and testing. Among these contributions were statistical concepts such as the correlation coefficient (Galton, 1894), methodological advances including the adoptive family (Galton, 1869) and twin study (Galton, 1875) methods, and the invention of questionnaire research (Galton, 1874). He was also the first person to use the phrase "nature and nurture" as a way of conceptualizing the relative roles of heredity and environment in shaping human nature (Galton, 1874). Galton was an unwavering proponent of the hereditarian position, using studies of family trees to attempt to prove that genius is biologically determined. Galton coined the term *eugenics* to describe his utopian vision for creating a superior strain of human beings through selective breeding. The concept of the intelligence test emerged from this eugenics application (Galton, 1883).

Darwin and *On the Origin of Species*

In 1859 Galton read *On the Origin of Species,* which had been recently published by his half-cousin Charles Darwin, and he was immediately captivated by evolutionary theory. He had previously established himself as an expert in researching the supposed psychological differences among cultural groups, and his ethnocentric views were not unlike those of many other British explorers of the Victorian era (Galton, 1861b; see also Fancher, 1983, 1985). However, Darwin's paradigm-shifting ideas provided a new way to think about these perceived psychological trends. Evolutionary theory suggested to him that psychological differences might be attributable to specific, inheritable characteristics of the brain and nervous system. Over time, natural selection would ensure that small inherited variations that contributed positively to human experience would become more common in specific populations, paralleling the process of natural selection of physical characteristics in the animal kingdom. Therefore, he reasoned, it might be possible to control the direction and speed of human evolution through carefully planned breeding (Fancher, 1983, 1985).

Armed with this Darwinian theoretical base, Galton began looking for evidence. In 1865 he published the article "Hereditary Talent and Character," in which he undertook a statistical investigation of biographical dictionary entries in an attempt to demonstrate empirically that talent runs in families. While acknowledging that the laws of inheritance were not well understood by the scientific community, he dismissed the importance of environmental influences on the characteristics he identified. This work was followed four years later by *Hereditary Genius: An Inquiry Into Its Laws and Consequences* (1869). This book applied the same line of reasoning as the earlier paper, but on a much larger scale, examining 1,000 eminent men from 300 families. Galton's statistical analysis showed here also that eminence does tend to run in families, and that this tendency is comparable to that of certain physical traits, such as extreme height, that were already acknowledged as being influenced by heredity. The book also used ethnic, racial, and national comparisons in an attempt to provide additional evidence that inherited psychological characteristics have a large-scale impact on societies (Fancher, 1983, 1985).

Flawed as it is, *Hereditary Genius* was a monumental contribution, serving as the first major empirical study of genius (Forrest, 1974; Simonton, 2009), and it set the stage for future generations of researchers interested in the developmental history of gifted and eminent individuals.[1]

Eugenics

Darwin's evolutionary theory suggested to Galton that it might be possible to exploit the principles of natural selection to purposefully direct the evolutionary progression of the human species. In 1883 he coined the term *eugenics,* from the Greek *eu* (good) and *genos* (birth), to describe this process. Galton was not the first to suggest that it was in the best interests of society for certain kinds of people to breed with one another, and for other kinds of people to abstain from having children. Precursors to modern eugenics had had been around since Plato's *Republic* (ca. 380 BCE). However, Galton was the first to use scientific principles to suggest a system for bringing eugenic goals to fruition.

Galton's vision was roughly as follows. Highly intelligent young men and women should be encouraged to intermarry and have many children; over time, this will increase the number of intellectually superior human beings in the general population. Galton hoped that the British government would help this process along by creating a national register of unmarried, highly gifted individuals—something he called the "golden book of natural nobility"—that could be used by young geniuses to find intellectually gifted mates (1873, p. 125). In his perfect world, the Queen of England herself would give away the brides in these marriages and bestow 5,000 pounds on each of the dutiful couples as a wedding present from the state (Galton, 1865). Eventually this intervention would not be needed, as young geniuses sympathetic to the cause would naturally seek each other out (Galton, 1873). At the same time, people of ordinary or subnormal intelligence would be discouraged from having children. Galton hoped that ordinary folks would see the wisdom of eugenics and voluntarily abstain from having children, and perhaps even choose to give some of the financial resources they saved from not raising children to help support large genius families. In this way, he radically redefined the concept of charity. He also recommended that traditional forms of charity be limited to those families who were willing to practice birth control (Galton, 1873; see also Fancher, 1983, 1985).

The Concept of the Intelligence Test

Galton came up with the concept of intelligence testing as a way to bring these eugenicist ideals to fruition. He recognized that the concept of the "golden book of natural nobility" was not ideal, because the intellectual eminence condition that Galton used to identify genius generally does not show itself until middle age. He needed a way to identify potential geniuses before they could pair off and start to have children.

To develop his test to detect young geniuses, Galton turned to anthropometry—literally, the measurement of humans. It made sense to him that because people take in information with their senses, those with the keenest senses must have the most efficient nervous systems. Therefore, he reasoned, intellectual capacity must be evident in measures of neurological efficiency. He created a series of tests to measure such things as reaction time, sensory acuity, and motor control (Galton, 1885a, 1885b; see also Fancher, 1983, 1985; Kaufman, 2009; Simonton, 2009). These anthropometric experiments were the first attempt at creating a scientific intelligence test (Kaufman, 2009).

Galton's data gathering strategy was brilliant. Instead of wasting time trying to recruit research participants to come to his laboratory, he brought his laboratory to them (Simonton, 2009). In 1884 he set up shop at the London International Health Exhibition, where the masses gladly offered threepence apiece for the privilege of being tested and receiving a written report of their performance. Over the next 6 years more than 9,000 people of varying ages were tested in Galton's laboratory, giving Galton a very large sample size and making him the first scientist to systematically study individual differences in the general population (Fancher, 1985; Gould, 1981; Kaufman, 2009). Along the way he also advanced the field of statistics by creating ways to determine the strength of a relationship between sets of his variables. His method was improved by his student Karl Pearson (1857–1936) and developed into the modern correlation coefficient—a fundamental statistical tool in many scientific fields.

Word of Galton's anthropometric testing spread to Wilhelm Wundt's experimental psychology laboratory in Germany, where it caught the attention of the American graduate student James McKeen Cattell (1860–1944). Impressed by Galton's work, Cattell arranged a 2-year research fellowship for himself in London. In 1888 he brought the anthropometry data back to the United States. It was here that anthropometry met its end. In the course of his dissertation research, Cattell's graduate student Clark Wissler (1870–1947) discovered that there were no meaningful correlations between any of Cattell's anthropometric variables and other external measures that might indicate degree of intelligence, such as grade point average in college (Wissler, 1901; see also Kaufman, 2009). At the time of Wissler's dissertation, anthropometric measurement was the primary research paradigm for intelligence testing. After Wissler's results became known, psychology gradually lost interest in psychophysical testing in favor of the more fruitful approach about to be developed in Paris by Alfred Binet (1857–1911) and Theodore Simon (1873–1961).

A BRIEF PSYCHOLOGICAL BIOGRAPHY OF GALTON

Early biographers often intimated that Galton saw himself as a genius, and that this vanity was one impetus for his professional interest in that topic (e.g., Forrest, 1974). Recently another view has emerged. It may be that Galton's intense focus on explaining the origins of genius in rigidly hereditary terms was at least in part derived from his need to explain certain unpleasant aspects of his own intellectual experience, rather than a compulsion to glorify his own accomplishments. This is the thesis put forth by the psychology historian Raymond Fancher, who describes Galton's writings as being at times "poignantly autobiographical" rather than self-aggrandizing (Fancher, 1985, p. 25; see also Fancher, 1983, 1998).

Galton was the younger half-cousin of Charles Darwin, born into the same affluent and venerable English family. He was a precocious child with wide-ranging interests and a penchant for memorizing whole passages of literature after just a few readings. His family was inordinately proud of these intellectual accomplishments, seeing them as foreshadowing his academic success. Galton's older sister, perpetually ill and with lots of time on her hands, made him her special project, bestowing extravagant attention on his education. He responded well, and his family soon proclaimed their confidence that he would be the first person from his father's side to earn a university degree, and the first of his family to achieve distinction at university. Young Galton internalized these weighty expectations, and as a very young child he stated that the thing he most wanted in the world was to receive university honors. (Before his fifth birthday he had begun saving money to purchase these honors.) Throughout childhood his family continued to remind him of his exceptionality, and he came to believe that this was his role in life—to be exceptional. As he grew older Galton cultivated this identity, seeking ongoing proof of this exceptionality by setting lofty academic goals and seeking conspicuous success in prestigious intellectual competitions (Fancher, 1983, 1985, 1998).

Unfortunately for this small boy with designs set on greatness, the early education his doting family had provided for him had not been focused on the right things. It certainly made for a good show (the young Galton was reading Shakespeare for house-guests by age 6), but it lacked the substance and discipline that was required for one to be competitive in the strict British boarding school he began attending at age 8. Although he was initially placed in a class with older students, he was quickly demoted. A series of other small indignities followed in short order. Far from being the academic star everyone had expected him to become, he revealed himself to be a "mediocre classical scholar [whose] diaries and letters reflected a dreary sequence of punitive assignments and feeble excuses for his failure to excel" (Fancher, 1985, p. 22). However, he retained his childhood ambition of proving his excellence, and by adolescence his competitive spirit was clearly evident in his letters to his father, in which he displayed his keen eye for sizing up the intellectual strengths and weaknesses of other students whom he viewed as his competition (Fancher, 1985).

This inauspicious beginning did not bode well for Galton's goal of achieving honors at university. By the time he matriculated to Cambridge at age 18, he had come to realize that his chances of earning honors in classics were slim, but he remained optimistic that he could earn honors in other areas. His family's unwavering confidence is unmistakable in a letter from his sister: "Father is building castles in the air that you will turn out so clever that you will have enough to spare for [your brothers] also" (E. Galton, 1840). Galton never scored high enough on his university examinations to earn honors, and for a brief time this disappointment caused him to collapse into a crippling emotional crisis. When he graduated in 1843, he received an ordinary, nonhonors degree, and he abandoned formal education altogether in 1844, when an inheritance from his father made it possible to do so.

For many years Galton drifted without purpose, sheltered by his wealth. He traveled to exotic places, honed his marksmanship skills, and played at the sport of ballooning. Still wounded by his university experience, he eventually sought counsel with a professional phrenologist, who confirmed that the shape of his head did not predispose him to scholarly success. The phrenologist—most likely equipped with some prior knowledge of Galton's background—advised his client that his brain was suited to a practical, active career. This phrenological examination would prove to be a positive turning point for Galton; his ambition and energy returned, now redirected toward more adventurous outdoor endeavors, which would ultimately bring him his first public acclaim (Fancher, 1983, 1985, 1998).

One must consider the possibility that a man such as Galton, supremely self-confident and greatly desiring of academic accolades, endowed with so many environmental advantages—social status, wealth, access to education, the capacity for industriousness, and the unshakable confidence of his family—would eventually conclude that geniuses are born rather than made (Fancher, 1983, 1985, 1998). His own life history seemed to demonstrate that there is, for each individual, a predetermined upper intellectual limit beyond which education and aspiration cannot help one to advance. He took the same courses as his more successful fellows at the boarding school and at Cambridge. He studied just as hard—or harder—than they did. He wanted success as much as anyone could. And yet he did not come out on top.

Fancher (1983, 1985, 1998) suggests that there is an important connection between these personal encounters with disappointment and Galton's apparent blindness to any possible environmental origins of genius. Consider the following passage from Galton's *Hereditary Genius* (1869):

> The eager boy, when he first goes to school and confronts intellectual difficulties, is astonished at his progress. He glories in his newly-developed mental grip and growing capacity for application, and, it may be, fondly believes it to be within his reach to become one of the heroes who have left their mark upon the history of the world. The years go by; he competes in the examinations of

school and college, over and over again with his fellows, and soon finds his place among them. He knows he can beat such and such of his competitors; that there are some with whom he runs on equal terms, and others whose intellectual feats he cannot even approach. (pp. 56–57)

Is the generalized "eager boy" of *Hereditary Genius* Francis Galton? Quite possibly. Galton's self-perceived failures had proved devastating to his sense of self until the phrenologist offered a supposedly "natural" explanation for them. Freed from trying to live up to familial expectations, Galton was finally at liberty to pursue his true genius. The ensuing years were characterized by a series of celebrated accomplishments, culminating in his major contributions to intelligence theory and testing. The price he paid for this ultimate success, however, was an inability to see alternatives to his strongly hereditarian position.

By almost any objective measure, Sir Francis Galton was an extraordinarily successful man. Knighted in 1909, he has been deemed a genius by posterity (Simonton, 2009). He developed the statistical concept of the correlation coefficient; conducted the first scientific study of genius; pioneered the adoptive family, twin study, and questionnaire research methods; and coined the scientific phrase "nature and nurture." His anthropometric testing laboratories brought the concept of intelligence testing to the world. Unfortunately, his a priori hereditarian assumptions prevented him from acknowledging the importance of mechanisms other than biological inheritance that were at work in his investigations of intelligence. His misguided focus on eugenics pollutes his legacy. His psychological biography sheds some light on these professional missteps, and may make the 21st-century reader a bit more sympathetic to his human flaws. In the end, scientists are not immune from having their personal experiences—both triumphs and failures—influence and bias their work.

TAKEAWAYS

- Sir Francis Galton was the first scientist to study genius in a systematic way.
- Galton coined the term *eugenics* to describe his utopian vision for creating a superior type of human being through selective breeding. He originated the idea of intelligence testing as a way to identify young geniuses for this program.
- Galton developed the statistical concept of the correlation coefficient and pioneered the adoptive family, twin study, and questionnaire research methods.
- An unwavering advocate of the hereditarian position, Galton was the first scientist to use the phrase "nature and nurture."
- Galton's personal struggle to attain academic honors may have influenced his belief that geniuses are born, not made.

NOTE

1. Readers who are interested in the study of genius in the 21st century should read Dean Keith Simonton's excellent contribution to the Psychology 101 series, *Genius 101* (2009).

4

The Best of Intentions: What Goddard Teaches Us About the Development of Intelligence (and the Rough-and-Tumble World of Science)

December 5, 1912

Dear Madam,

We have good news for you. The results of the intelligence test administered to your brother indicate that he is not an

(continued)

(*continued*)
imbecile, as we first suspected. He is actually a moron, which is a higher grade of mental defective. I'm sure you are relieved to hear this news! He is welcome at our institution for feeble-minded persons. We are confident that we can train him to be self-sustaining and to avoid the fate of other degenerates who are left to their own devices in society. While his mental age of 9 years old is far below his actual age of 20, he has greater potential for training than the 20-year-old idiots and imbeciles who live at our institution (although, of course, we do our best to help them also). Please let us know if you have further questions.

Warmest regards,
Dr. Jones, Psychologist
Acme Institution for Feeble-Minded Persons

No doubt you are appalled by the fictitious letter presented above. No special educator or psychologist would ever use such language to describe a person with an intellectual disability . . . or would they? The letter itself is not real, but its tenor, sentiment, and vocabulary are entirely consistent with early-20th-century attitudes toward individuals with compromised intellectual functioning. Indeed, an educated reader of the time would likely be impressed by the cutting-edge science used in diagnosing this person. Of course, we created this letter with shock value in mind— but you may be even more horrified by some of the real quotes presented later in this chapter. Henry Herbert Goddard's (1866–1957) legacy is a complicated one, populated by great triumphs that advanced the utility and accessibility of intelligence testing in the United States, and by professional missteps that make 21st-century intelligence researchers cringe.[1] Our goal in this chapter is to present a balanced overview of the man and his work to illustrate the complicated history of intelligence theory and testing.

GETTING USED TO THE VOCABULARY

Before diving into Goddard's story, we need to desensitize you to some of the vocabulary used in this chapter. When we teach classes about intelligence theory and testing, many students struggle with the terms that Goddard and many of his contemporaries used. One of us (Amber) vividly remembers the first time she opened Goddard's 1912 book, *The Kallikak Family: A Study in the Heredity of Feeble-Mindedness*, and recoiled at the unabashed use of terms such as *idiot, imbecile,* and *moron*. What she did not know then is that these terms were not intended to be insulting. At first they were imprecise clinical labels used to describe physicians' and teachers' subjective judgments of intellectual ability levels. They eventually became technical classifications that described lower-functioning individuals' performance on Henry Goddard's English translation of the Binet–Simon (1908) intelligence test.

In 1904 the French government commissioned a group of experts to create a mechanism for identifying low-achieving students who would benefit from special education services. In 1905 Alfred Binet (1857–1911) and his student Theodore Simon (1873–1961) responded by publishing the Binet–Simon scale, arguably the world's first intelligence test (see the extensive discussion in Kaufman, 2009). The test consisted of a series of 30 tasks of increasing complexity. Some of the simplest test items assessed whether or not a child could follow a lit match with his eyes or shake hands with the examiner. Slightly harder tasks required children to point to various named body parts, to repeat a series of three digits or a simple sentence given by the administrator, and to define words such as *house, fork,* and *mama*. More difficult test items required children to state the difference between pairs of things, to reproduce drawings from memory, and to construct sentences from three given words, such as *Paris, river,* and *fortune.* The hardest items asked children to repeat a provided sequence of seven random digits, to find three rhymes for the French word *obéissance,* and to answer questions such as "My neighbor has been receiving strange visitors. He has received in turn a doctor, a lawyer, and then a priest. What is taking place?" (Fancher, 1985).

These tasks were carefully calibrated to reveal each child's "mental level," which could then be compared with his or her chronological age. For example, a 10-year-old child who completed all the tasks usually completed by 10-year-olds—but nothing beyond those tasks—would have a mental level that exactly matched his or her chronological age, 10.0. A child assigned a mental level 2 or more years behind her chronological age (e.g., a 10-year-old child with a mental level of 8.0) was generally diagnosed as being mentally subnormal (Fancher, 1985).

Goddard and the Binet–Simon Scale

Goddard brought the Binet–Simon scale to the United States and translated it into English, replacing *mental level* with *mental age.* The fictitious 20-year-old brother described in the letter at the start of this chapter would have been given the label *moron* because his mental age—based on the Binet intelligence test— was somewhere been ages 8 and 12 years. His less fortunate peers, the imbeciles, would have had mental ages somewhere between 3 and 7, and the idiots below 3. *Feeble-minded* was the original term for the highest of the low-performing groups (replaced by *moron* in 1910), but the descriptor came to be an all-encompassing term that confounded low intellectual functioning with other problems including epilepsy, substance abuse, and evidence of moral deficiency. Other terms, such as *laggard, degenerate, cretin, mental deficient,* and *cripple,* were also used freely by Goddard and his early-20th-century contemporaries in the professional literature (Zenderland, 1998).

Before you pass judgment on Goddard and his compatriots for their insensitivity, it is important to understand that the professional language of psychology is constantly evolving. Consider the label *mentally retarded*. As we write this (in mid-2013) it is considered very impolite[2] to call someone "retarded." However, up until 2007 the major research and advocacy group supporting people with cognitive deficits was called the American Association on Mental Retardation (now the American Association on Intellectual and Developmental Disabilities) (Schalock et al., 2010). The word *retarded* can be traced back to the 12th-century French word *retarder*, which means "to delay, protract, or be slow" (Oxford English Dictionary, 2011). In its fundamental form—stripped of sociological context—the term *mentally retarded* simply means that one attribute of the individual is that he or she learns at a slower pace compared with most others. This may actually be helpful or necessary information for a psychologist, teacher, or physician who is trying to help that person.

But it is impossible to ignore the sociological context, of course. *Retarded* should no longer be used to describe people. This label, once employed by professionals as a convenient shorthand to describe slow learning, has been appropriated by the general public and turned into an insult. Once children started calling other kids "retards" on the playground, science needed to come up with a new descriptive term. This term would have to be devoid of stereotypes and reflect the most recent, research-based understandings about this constellation of disorders. The labels now preferred by the American Association on Intellectual and Developmental Disability are *intellectual disability* and *person with an intellectual disability*. In addition to replacing any reference to retardation, these new descriptors put the most important thing (that he or she is a person) first, subordinating the attribute to second place: She is not an intellectually disabled person. She is a person with an intellectual disability (Schalock, Luckasson, & Shogren, 2007). This change was codified in 2010 when President

Obama signed Rosa's Law (2010; Public Law 111-256), mandating that the phrases *mental retardation* and *mentally retarded* be removed from federal health, education, and labor policy and replaced with *intellectual disability* and *person with an intellectual disability*. Likewise, the newest version of the *Diagnostic and Statistical Manual of Mental Disorders* has replaced the category "Mental Retardation" with "Intellectual Developmental Disability" (American Psychiatric Association, 2013).

For now, *person with an intellectual disability* works. But it is difficult to stop society from usurping professional labels. Perhaps in a few years these new descriptors will leak onto the playground as well, with some kids taunting other kids, "You're such an intell-dis" or some such nonsense.[3] Someday psychologists and special educators will have to choose new terms to describe specific attributes of individuals with low intelligence scores and poor adaptive functioning. It might be useful to ponder this possibility as you read on about Henry Herbert Goddard.

GODDARD'S CONTRIBUTIONS TO AMERICAN INTELLIGENCE THEORY AND TESTING

Goddard coined the term *moron* in 1910 to signify the highest group of mentally deficient people (Goddard, 1910). In arguing for this change, he hoped to encourage precision in classifying individuals with compromised intellectual functioning. This search for precision is one of his greatest contributions to the fields of intelligence theory and testing. It is, in fact, the reason intelligence testing became available in the United States.

When Goddard came on the scene as the new Director of Research at the Training School for Feeble-Minded Girls and Boys in Vineland, New Jersey, in 1906, there was no agreed-upon system for defining, diagnosing, and classifying intellectual disability.

This is important because it is very hard to help someone if you don't know the nature of his or her difficulties. In Goddard's time, specialists routinely relied on a subjective, "we know it when we see it" approach, resulting in unreliable evaluations of intellectual ability and inconsistent prognoses for improvement. Having spent considerable time with more than 300 students at the Vineland school, Goddard believed that some people who worked closely with disabled persons could be relied on to make "rather accurate" intuitive judgments about intellectual ability (Goddard, 1908b, p. 12). However, he also knew that an objective scientific method was necessary to advance psychological science. Earlier attempts at this task by other researchers had failed (Zenderland, 1998).

Goddard experimented with several approaches to mental testing for 2 years (in what would become the first laboratory for the scientific study of intellectual disability), but without meaningful results (Zenderland, 1998). In 1908 Goddard took an extended trip to Europe seeking counsel with experts there. He met extensively with prominent psychologists and visited physicians and teachers. On one visit a Belgian physician and special educator named Ovide Decroly handed Goddard a copy of the Binet–Simon intelligence test (Binet & Simon, 1905). This approach to mental testing was entirely different from anything that had been tried before. Intrigued by its possibilities, Goddard brought the test back to the United States and tried the tasks with the students at the Vineland school. A subsequent article by Binet and Simon (1908) provided a full test battery that used typical children between the ages of 3 and 13 as the norm. This made it possible to compare any given child's score against the norm and come up with an approximate "mental level" for that child.

Goddard translated the Binet test and administered it to all of his Vineland students. He noted with pleasure that the mental ages of the children based on their test scores generally corresponded to the intuitive judgments made by the Vineland staff, providing evidence of criterion validity. Using mental age as a primitive sort of cut-score, he was now able to distinguish idiots, imbeciles, and morons. Finally, he had attained the diagnostic precision that physicians, psychologists, and special educators had been trying for! Goddard wrote about this endeavor in his institution's journal, and with this publication he introduced the United States to the first real intelligence test (Goddard, 1908a; see also Kaufman, 2009; Zenderland, 1998). Soon thereafter, the American Association for the Study of the Feeble-Minded tentatively adopted Goddard's classification system as "the most reliable method at present in use for determining the mental status of feeble-minded children" (Rogers, 1910). With this adoption, intelligence testing became firmly entrenched in American society (Zenderland, 1998).

In the following years Goddard made several significant contributions that advanced intelligence testing. In 1911 he was invited to bring intelligence testing to the New York City school district—the nation's largest, at 75,000 students (Zenderland, 1998). By 1915 he had distributed 22,000 copies of the Binet test and 88,000 answer blanks throughout the United States (Fancher, 1985). He was a vocal advocate for public school special education, and in 1911 he helped write the first state law mandating special education classes for children with disabilities. This law stipulated that school districts had to create a special class whenever they had 10 or more students who were performing at a level 3 years behind their chronological ages. Thus, Binet's concept of mental age was granted de facto recognition in state law. Goddard was also very forward-thinking in arguing that convicted criminals who had subnormal intelligence scores should not be executed (Zenderland, 1998). This principle became law in 2002 with *Atkins v. Virginia*, which stipulated that convicted defendants who are mentally retarded cannot be executed, as this would violate the Eighth Amendment ban on cruel and unusual punishment.

In 1917 Goddard joined the American Psychological Association's Committee on the Psychological Examination of Recruits. As part of this team he helped to construct two versions of the world's first group intelligence test, which was designed to help the U.S. Army identify recruits with low intelligence and recognize soldiers who were particularly suited for special assignments and officer training schools (McGuire, 1994). By the end of the First World War, this test had been administered to approximately 2 million men. The publicity generated by this program popularized the idea of intelligence testing and provided vast amounts of data that could be used by intelligence researchers for future work (Fancher, 1985; Larson, 1994; McGuire, 1994). Unfortunately for the United States, the test results indicated that 45% of the healthy young men being considered for military service scored in the feeble-minded range. This surprising result raised questions about the test's diagnostic accuracy and was instrumental in changing some of Goddard's views later in his career (Goddard, 1927).

GODDARD'S CONTROVERSIES

Despite his many significant contributions to the fields of intelligence testing and special education, Goddard is probably remembered most for the controversies he engendered during his long career. Believing that feeble-mindedness was an inherited characteristic, he aligned himself with the American eugenics movement—a group populated by powerful and influential individuals who believed that the genetic quality of the U.S. population could be improved through social and political means (Black, 2003). One particular worry of eugenicists was that the feeble-minded would breed and pass on their infirmity, making the U.S. population less intelligent with each successive generation. Goddard was among those who argued in favor of compulsory segregation or sterilization of feeble-minded individuals. He was also instrumental in developing a program to prevent idiots, imbeciles, and morons from entering the United States through the Ellis Island checkpoint (see Fancher, 1985; Gould, 1981; Zenderland, 1998). This section of the chapter will explore these controversial aspects of Goddard's legacy.

When Goddard began his work with the students at the Vineland school, his research focused on the psychological and educational problems associated with feeble-minded people. He was interested in pedagogy, and he was optimistic about the development of new teaching methods that might improve the lives of his students. As his career advanced, however, his research interests expanded into the larger biological and social implications of feeble-mindedness. On the recommendation of a colleague, he began reading about Mendelian theory. Unfortunately, he misunderstood the concepts and began to think of feeble-mindedness as a single recessive hereditary trait. For him, intelligence ceased to be a continuum from less smart to more smart, and was transformed into a binary quality: Either you had it or you did not. And you passed on what you had to your children (Goddard, 1912a; see also Fancher, 1985; Gould, 1981; Zenderland, 1998).

In 1912 Goddard published his first major work tackling the problem of what he called "defective ancestry." *The Kallikak Family: A Study in the Heredity of Feeble-Mindedness* (Goddard, 1912a) chronicled the family history of one of his Vineland students, a young woman who had been sent to live at the institution when she was 8 years old. Goddard gave her the name Deborah Kallikak, a pseudonym created from the Greek words *kallos* (beauty) and *kakos* (bad). This unusual surname represents the union of beauty and badness that Goddard believed he had discovered in her family line. He was able to trace her lineage back six generations to an 18th-century union between a young Revolutionary War soldier he named Martin Kallikak and an unnamed, feeble-minded girl whom the soldier met in a local tavern. Their union produced a single son. The *kakos* (bad) branch of his family descended from this affair, yielding generation after generation of feeble-minded individuals. Later, Martin Kallikak married a Quaker woman from a good family and had a second son by his new wife. The socially and economically successful members of the *kallos* (beautiful) branch of the family descended from this marriage.

Goddard believed that the Kallikak family provided a perfect natural experiment, the result of which established the importance of heredity in determining feeble-mindedness. The profound difference between the two sides of the family was believed to be conclusive proof of its hereditary nature: two different types of women, two different types of hereditary endowments. He was blind to the many weaknesses in his methodology, notably that in searching for evidence of feeble-mindedness in family trees he confounded low intelligence with other conditions, including alcoholism, epilepsy, the tendency to have children outside of marriage, and criminal behavior. Moreover, he dismissed the many environmental influences that were at work in shaping the generations on both sides of the Kallikak family. The book gave the impression of a major scientific breakthrough, however, drawing relatively little professional criticism and earning him an international reputation as a leading expert on mental deficiency. It was also a tremendous hit with the public and was reprinted several times over the ensuing decades (Zenderland, 1998). Subsequent generations of scholars have been far less enthusiastic about Goddard's methodology and his conclusions, of course, with some even suggesting that he doctored photographs of the "bad" side of the Kallikak family to make them appear more sinister (see Gould, 1981). However, most scholars now reject this idea, inasmuch as this would be counterproductive to Goddard's belief that, to the untrained eye, "morons" look just like the rest of us (Zenderland, 1998)—hence the need for intellectual testing.

GODDARD'S RECOMMENDATIONS

Goddard was convinced that he could not cure feeble-mindedness, but he had several suggestions for preventing it. One potential solution was involuntary sterilization of feeble-minded people. The feeble-minded, he warned, were "multiplying at twice the rate of the general population" (1912a, p. 71) and were producing "more feeble-minded children with which to clog the wheels of human progress" (1912a, p. 78). Over time, this would result in a noticeable decrease in U.S. national intelligence.[4] Compulsory ovariectomy and castration procedures would prevent this gradual decline (1912a, p. 107). He noted that, in males, "the operation itself is almost as simple . . . as having a tooth pulled. In females it is not much more serious" (1912a, p. 108).[5] Prominent eugenicists had already argued for compulsory sterilization, so Goddard was aware that it was an unpopular idea:

> There are two great practical difficulties in the way of carrying out this method on any large scale. The first is the strong opposition to this practice on the part of the public generally. It is regarded as mutilation of the human body and as such is opposed vigorously by many people. And while there is no rational basis for this, nevertheless we have, as practical reformers, to recognize the fact that the average man acts not upon reason, but upon sentiment and feeling; and as long as human sentiment and feeling are opposed to this practice, no amount of reasoning will avail. (Goddard, 1912a, p. 107)

Given the voiced objections to sterilization, Goddard felt that humane colonization would be a more practical solution. Inmates could be segregated by sex, and this would accomplish the same eugenic aims. In Goddard's paternalistic view, segregation had an advantage over sterilization in that it protected the inmates as well as society. As he explained it, a feeble-minded woman who was left to her own devices in society was destined to become "prey to the designs of evil men or evil women and . . . lead a life that would be vicious, immoral, and criminal, though because of her mentality she herself would not be responsible" (Goddard, 1912a, p.12). Safely ensconced in a colony, she would do no harm to others, and others could not unduly influence or harm her.

Goddard's colonies never manifested in the way he envisioned them, but some institutions experimented with alternative forms of adult custodial care. One such experiment was the "farm colonies," communities of feeble-minded adults who worked the land and raised livestock using state-of-the-art agricultural techniques. The farm colony associated with Goddard's Vineland school had a research partnership with Rutgers University and was very successful in developing new methods of growing peaches, raising chickens, and improving egg production. Despite their apparent success in many areas, the colonies were not self-supporting and required a substantial influx of cash from the state (Zenderland, 1998). His recommendations about sterilization were more successful: In subsequent years, 30 states adopted compulsory sterilization programs. The last of these were shut down in the 1970s (see Hyatt, 1997; Silver, 2003; cf. Schoen, 2001).

Immigration Restriction

From 1890 to 1910 more than 12 million immigrants boarded ships headed for the New World. Immigration critics in the United States warned that those who made up this massive influx were "less educated, more impoverished, and more culturally 'alien' than earlier groups of immigrants" (Zenderland, 1998, p. 263). These fears led to a resurgence of interest in immigration restriction. In 1882 the U.S. Congress passed a law prohibiting "idiots" and "lunatics" from passing through the Ellis Island checkpoint. By 1903 Congress had similarly banned the insane, epileptics, beggars, and anarchists. By 1907 the law included imbeciles, feeble-minded persons, and those with physical or mental defects that might prevent them from sustaining themselves through employment (Zenderland, 1998).

Goddard often gets the blame for many of these policies, but it is worth noting that some of the laws predate his work somewhat significantly. That said, in 1910 he was asked by immigration officials to lend his expertise to their efforts to enforce them. Enforcement had proven difficult, as thousands upon thousands of people were passing through the checkpoint at Ellis Island every day. It is important to note that the officials' pleas for urgency in this matter frequently degenerated into warnings about racial inferiority, but Goddard did not share these views. He had never designed a study comparing native-born with foreign-born children, or compared the intelligence of Caucasians with that of another group. Unlike many of his contemporaries, he didn't mention race, ethnicity, or religion when writing articles about feeble-minded schoolchildren.

Nevertheless, Goddard agreed to come to Ellis Island. The procedure he developed in 1912 was a two-step process: One assistant would visually screen for suspected mental defectives as the immigrants passed through the checkpoint. These individuals would then proceed to another location, where the other assistant would test them using a variety of performance measures and a revised version of the Binet scales, often aided by an interpreter. Goddard believed that trained inspectors would be more accurate than the Ellis Island physicians; the key to their success was expertise developed through extended experience with feeble-minded people: In one of his most memorable quotes, he likened the process of detecting feeble-mindedness to wine or tea tasting (Zenderland, 1998, p. 268).[6]

The results of this mental testing program were startling. In *Intelligence Classification of Immigrants of Different Nationalities* (Goddard, 1917), he asserted that most of the Ellis Island immigrants were mentally deficient. For example, he indicated that 83% of all Jews tested were feeble-minded, as were 80% of the Hungarians,[7] 79% of the Italians, and 87% of the Russians. Significantly, Goddard was far more willing to entertain the theory attributing environmental causes for these results than he had been with his native-born American students. Some immigrants, he acknowledged, had "never had a pen or pencil in their hands." Why, then, should they do well on a task requiring them to draw a test item from memory (Goddard, 1917)? Keeping this in mind, he decided to throw out any Binet questions that were failed by 75% of the immigrants tested. The new version of his test drastically reduced the number of potential immigrants who were diagnosed as feeble-minded. But even in acknowledging the fairness of this new system, he worried about the consequences for the United States. Environmentally caused feeble-mindedness would not be passed to offspring via sexual reproduction, but the new test standard seemed much too low for prospective Americans who were going to live out their lives within our borders (Goddard, 1917). Regardless of any reliance on environmental explanations, the number of immigrants who were deported increased exponentially as a result of Goddard's screening measures (Zenderland, 1998).

GODDARD'S MODIFIED VIEWS

By the late 1920s Goddard had revised many of his early opinions, declaring in multiple public forums that he had been gravely mistaken in assuming that anyone who tested below a mental age of 12 was feeble-minded. By the end of his career, he had come to believe that "only a small percentage" of people who had previously been diagnosed as feeble-minded were in fact mentally deficient (Goddard, 1928, p. 220). One reason for this change of heart was his participation in the development of group intelligence tests prior to the First World War:

> The war led to the measurement of the intelligence of the drafted army, with the result that such an enormous proportion was found to have an intelligence of 12 years and less that to call them all feebleminded was an absurdity of the highest degree. Of 1,700,000 soldiers tested, 45% did not get above the 12-year limit. Inasmuch as 1,700,000 men were a fair sample of the entire population, we conclude that these figures hold for the people of the country . . . it is evident that these people are not morons. (Goddard, 1927, p. 42)

Goddard also recanted his early statements that feeble-mindedness was incurable. The condition itself could not be reversed, but the symptoms could be relieved through education. He had seen evidence in many institutions that feeble-minded people could "be trained to become self-supporting and capable of managing [their own affairs]" (Goddard, 1927, p. 44). He was now much more amenable to permitting them to go out into the world. The danger of allowing unchecked breeding was mitigated by certain advantages—specifically, that feeble-minded people were useful to the rest of society (Goddard, 1927).

This new, more "progressive" perspective on the problem of feeble-mindedness is still jarring to the 21st-century reader. Goddard never moved far enough away from his earlier statements to gain absolution. Perhaps the most devastating outcome of this work for Goddard and for the world came just a few years after he began publishing his revised views. The German translation of his book, *Die Familie Kallikak*, had been printed in Germany in 1914. The Nazi government reprinted it in 1933 and began using it in their propaganda. Nothing in any of Goddard's writings suggests that he intended his work to be used in this way.

In fact, on at least one occasion he used his fame to work against the Nazi cause, consistent with numerous actions during his career to support Jewish academics.

Goddard is often portrayed in the literature as a eugenic monster, but it is important to acknowledge that he was either a leader or a participant in every significant event involving the birth of American intelligence research and testing (Zenderland, 1998). He started the first scientific laboratory devoted to the study of people with intellectual disabilities, translated the Binet–Simon intelligence scale into English and distributed it widely, and convinced his colleagues to adopt intelligence testing as the gold standard for classifying individuals who were not learning normally. Far ahead of his time, he argued against capital punishment for people with subnormal intelligence. He advocated for special education classes in public schools and helped craft the first state law mandating these special classes. Indeed, he devoted his life to helping people with developmental disabilities.

However, Goddard was also a strong believer in the hereditarian position on intelligence, and given this time period's limited understanding of Mendelian genetics, he got most of it wrong. He argued in favor of segregation and compulsory sterilization of people with intellectual disabilities. By mid-career he had abandoned his drive for precision in mental testing, advocating for the acquired ability to detect feeble-mindedness at a glance, which he compared to wine or tea tasting. He recommended limiting immigration to people who would score well on intelligence tests. He referred to people with intellectual disabilities as mental defectives or degenerates, and classified them into the (now) offensive-sounding grades of idiot, imbecile, and moron. Arguably not a racist (the "bad" side of the Kallikak family were "white, Anglo-Saxon Protestants who had been living in America since the time of the Revolution"; Zenderland, 179, p. 124) or a transparent anti-Semite, he was undoubtedly a classist who never really understood the lives of the poor and working-class people who represented the "bad" side of the Kallikaks, or the feeble-minded immigrants at Ellis Island.

He was wise enough, however, to take stock at the end of his career and admit that he had made mistakes. Taken as a whole, Goddard's life is a study in contradictions. There is no doubt, however, that the fields of intelligence theory and testing would not be the same without his contributions—for better or for worse.

TAKEAWAYS

- Goddard started the first scientific laboratory devoted to the study of people with intellectual disabilities. He also translated the Binet–Simon (1908) intelligence scale into English and distributed it widely in the United States
- Goddard argued against capital punishment for people with subnormal intelligence and helped create the first state law mandating special education classes.
- Goddard argued in favor of segregation and compulsory sterilization of people with intellectual disabilities and assisted with a government program to limit immigration to the United States by individuals with subnormal intelligence.
- Goddard's career raises questions about the extent to which scientists are responsible for assisting or resisting government programs in their fields of expertise.

NOTES

1. The fact that Goddard was the University of Southern California's first football coach may also make some Notre Dame and UCLA fans cringe.

2. To put it mildly.
3. This is already happening. SPED is the prefix used by many universities for teacher preparation courses about special education; the spouse of one of the authors recalls hearing less-popular classmates called "speds" on the playground. Some universities now use the prefix EDSP. That is much harder to say, so it is less likely to be used as a taunt.
4. The tendency for high-IQ mothers to have fewer children than lower-IQ mothers is in fact an established finding in the 21st century. This so-called dysgenic fertility seems to be counterbalanced by the Flynn effect, which we describe in Chapter 6. For more information, see Lynn and Harvey (2008).
5. Ouch.
6. To this day, there are arguments for the value of asking intelligence test administrators to use their experience and clinical judgment, in addition to empirical tests, in the evaluation of intelligence. For more information, see Silverman (2012).
7. The first author, who proudly has Magyar blood coursing through his veins, humbly points to Joe Namath, Andy Grove, William Shatner, and Drew Barrymore as evidence that Hungarians rock it out.

Intelligence or
Intelligences?

p to this point, we have explored much of the early history of intelligence research. In Chapter 1 we briefly mentioned Spearman and his work, which occurred in parallel with that of Cattell, Binet, and Goddard. In this chapter we will describe Spearman's work, perhaps among the most influential in all of psychology, in some depth. Then we will show how psychologists developed and advanced their views of intelligence over much of the 20th century, roughly through the present day.

Much of this chapter focuses on arguments over whether intelligence is one thing or many things. This debate may seem trivial to the casual observer, but as Tyler (1969, p. v) notes, "[T]he question of whether intelligence is a unitary trait or only a name for a combination of loosely related, separately developed aptitudes for special kinds of thinking . . . is not a trivial one. What we think about this will influence our decisions about many other things, such as school policies, employment and unemployment, and the meaning of political equality." In other words, if you don't answer the "single versus multiple" question, it's hard to answer fairly routine questions, such as "Is this person talented?" or "Is this piece of work of high quality?" It is a fundamental question for a wide variety of domains—education, business, law, social justice, and many, many others.

SPEARMAN AND G

Let's travel back in time a little more than 100 years and start our discussion with the story of the British psychologist Charles Spearman. He came to psychology rather late in life, not beginning his studies in Wundt's famous psychology lab until he was in his 30s (his autobiography [1930] is highly recommended). Yet he quickly became an eminent psychologist, in large part due to his use of statistical evidence to support his ideas. He has been called the "first systematic psychometrician" and is considered to be the father of classical test theory (Jensen, 1994).

In this section we will focus on his work, beginning with his seminal 1904 paper, "'General Intelligence' Objectively Determined and Measured," which was published while he was still studying for his doctorate in Germany.[1] This paper looms so large in the history of intelligence that we use it, somewhat arbitrarily, to mark the beginning of the historical period we've labeled "The Great Schools' Influence."

Written partly in response to the debates surrounding the anthropometric research of Cattell, Wissler, and others around the dawn of the 20th century, Spearman (1904) proposed taking a very different approach to intelligence theory:

As regards the delicate matter of estimating "Intelligence," the guiding principle has been not to make any *a priori* assumptions as to what kind of mental activity may be thus termed with greatest propriety. Provisionally, at any rate, the aim was empirically to examine all the various abilities having any *prima facie* claims to such title, ascertaining their relations to one another and to other functions. (Spearman, 1904, pp. 249–250)

In other words, rather than define intelligence and then go looking for it, why not consider all abilities that could be used to describe intelligence, then create good measures of those abilities and take advantage of advances in statistics to determine how those abilities are related? This may sound like a matter of semantics, but Spearman's approach actually represented a major shift in how psychologists study the construct of intelligence.

Horn and McArdle (2007) go even further, crediting Spearman with using a more scientific approach than did his predecessors:

Spearman's theory . . . described what the results of doable experiments would be if the theory was correct—and, just as important, what the results would be if the theory was not correct. It required that one identify intelligence, whatever it was, and distinguish it from what was not intelligence. Spearman's theory thus directed the fledgling field of psychology toward research that could build a science to describe what people referred to when they used the term, *human intelligence.* (Horn & McArdle, 2007, p. 206, italics in original)

Spearman did revisit the work of Galton and others in an effort to reanalyze their results with more advanced statistical and psychometric techniques, many of which he pioneered. In particular, Spearman noted a number of statistical and methodological limitations in the work of Galton, Cattell, and Wissler. As mentioned earlier, there were no statistically meaningful relationships among Galton's and Cattell's mental tests, suggesting that the tasks were measuring a wide range of abilities. However, Spearman was able to demonstrate that these results were primarily due to reliability issues and restriction of range, and when he addressed these issues statistically, he achieved very different results from those of earlier researchers.

Indeed, not only did he find positive correlations among all the variables measured by the mental tests, he also found that those scores correlated with other mental ability measures. He was able to demonstrate that a common source of variance accounted for the correlations among all the mental tests, and he called this the general factor of intelligence, or g. Put more technically, he believed that a common factor was shared across most mental measures (g), and that each measure also had a specific factor (s) unique to that measure—hence the label *two-factor theory*, although the main thrust of this conceptualization is the existence of one general intellectual factor.

This finding reinvigorated the idea that intelligent behavior arises from a single metaphorical entity, and it forms the foundation for many present-day theories of human intelligence (see Jensen, 1994, 1998, for additional background). Over the ensuing decades, Spearman (1923; Spearman & Jones, 1950) and hundreds of other researchers (if not thousands!) conducted studies that largely supported the existence and importance of g. Jensen (1998) provides a comprehensive review of correlates with g, including a range of biological traits (body size, brain size, near-sightedness, brain activity), cognitive behaviors (reaction time, memory, learning ability), attainment (academic achievement, job performance), and important social outcomes (crime, divorce, mortality). Indeed, in a summary of current research on intelligence, Sternberg and Kaufman (2012) concluded that a recent decline in research on correlates of g is probably due to the fact that the relationship between g and a wide range of human behaviors is already well established.

However, that is not to say that Spearman's work has not been heavily criticized, both in his time (e.g., Burt, 1909; Thomson, 1939) and more recently (see Horn & McArdle, 2007, for a good review). As a case in point, we would be remiss if we didn't mention Herrnstein and Murray's controversial book, *The Bell Curve*, published in 1994. The book, with its defense and application of *g*, provoked a great deal of debate, in part because it appeared during an era dominated by theories proposing multiple intelligences (described below). If nothing else (and in contrast to, say, the work of Galton), you have to give the authors credit for swimming against the current so aggressively. Scholars who traditionally criticized unitary theories or psychometric approaches generally dismissed the book, yet many researchers supported the book's unitary, psychometric approach and conclusions about human ability—although many of those same supporters distanced themselves from the material on social implications, which was generally viewed as rather eugenic in nature. The heated debate about the book, which dominated public discourse in the United States for months, provided evidence that many psychologists remain supportive of unitary, psychometric theories of intelligence (see Gottfredson, 1997; Gottfredson et al., 1994).

THURSTONE'S THEORY OF PRIMARY MENTAL ABILITIES

The American psychologist L. L. Thurstone was active from just after the First World War until his death in 1955. Thurstone was interested in human problem solving, and he was a very talented statistician and psychometrician (the psychometric lab he created at the University of North Carolina is named after him). He also became interested in human intelligence, and although one of his early books is largely conceptual (Thurstone, 1924/1973), his later, empirical work resulted in the theory of primary mental abilities (PMA), consisting of word fluency, verbal comprehension, spatial visualization, number facility, associative memory, reasoning, and perceptual speed (Thurstone, 1938).

In his autobiography, Thurstone (1952) describes his interest and approach to intelligence as being a reaction to Spearman's work:

> [T]here was a quarter of a century of debate about Spearman's single factor method. . . . Throughout that debate over several decades, the orientation was to Spearman's general factor, and secondary attention was given to the group factors and specific factors which were frankly called "the disturbers of *g*." . . . The development of multiple-factor analysis consisted essentially in asking the fundamental question in a different way. Starting with an experimentally given table of correlation coefficients for a set of variables, we did not ask whether it supported any one general factor. We asked instead how many factors must be postulated in order to account for the observed correlations. At the very start of an analysis we faced very frankly the question as to how many factors must be postulated, and it should then be left as a question of fact in each inquiry whether one of these factors should be regarded as general. (p. 314)[2]

Thurstone argued that *g* was a statistical artifact resulting from the procedures used to study it, which produced an unhelpful average of multiple, specific intelligences (and provided little assistance in guiding future educational and vocational interventions; see Thurstone, 1936). Using a different approach to factor analysis that he had developed, Thurstone (1946) found evidence that intelligent behavior emerges from multiple factors rather than a unitary factor. When the correlations among the multiple factors were analyzed, they produced a number of higher-order factors, which included *g* (but not, as some have asserted, only *g*). As Thurstone (1952) described it near the end of his career:

> The correlations of the primary factors can be factored, just like the correlations among tests. When this is done we find several

second-order factors. One of these seems to agree very well with Spearman's general intellective factor *g*. The critics feature our support of Spearman's *g*, but they ignore the fact that this work represents at least a modest gain in unraveling the complexities of mental organization. (p. 316)

WECHSLER'S ASSESSMENT APPROACH

David Wechsler's considerable contributions are covered in more depth elsewhere (e.g., Kaufman, 2009) and are more pertinent to discussions of testing than to those of theory.[3] We mention him briefly here because he essentially proposed a two-factor, psychometrically derived model of intelligence. If you took an intelligence test in the second half of the 20th century, odds are you are personally familiar with Wechsler's work.

Wechsler is best known for developing several widely used intelligence tests, including the Wechsler Intelligence Scale for Children (Wechsler, 1949) and the Wechsler Adult Intelligence Scale (Wechsler, 1939), with new versions of these tests remaining popular today. Wechsler joined the U.S. Army testing teams during the First World War, where he worked with leading scholars such as Henry Goddard and Lewis Terman. He was later assigned to work with Spearman and Pearson in England during the waning months of the war.

Wechsler eventually concluded that Spearman's theory of general intelligence was too narrow. Unlike Spearman, Wechsler (1940) viewed intelligence as an effect rather than a cause and asserted that nonintellective factors, such as personality, contribute to the development of each person's intelligence. This "cause versus effect" issue sets Wechsler apart from many of the prominent intelligence scholars of his era. His personal definition, "Intelligence is the aggregate or global capacity of the individual to act purposefully, to think rationally and to deal effectively with his environment," reflects this broader view (Edwards, 1994; Wechsler, 1940, p. 3). Mirroring the U.S. Army Alpha and Beta tests, Wechsler's tests generally had two sets of tasks, one performance based and one dealing with verbal activities. Given the widespread use of his assessments, his performance and verbal differentiation was quite influential on how psychologists and educators came to view intelligence, although some scholars caution against viewing this differentiation as an attempt to assess two different types of ability, which was not Wechsler's intent (see Naglieri & Ford, in press).

CH AND SOMETIMES C THEORY[4]

At a major psychology conference in 1941, Raymond Cattell (no relation to James McKeen Cattell) reviewed the work in intelligence research and theory over the preceding decades. He observed, "Owing to the war the problem of adult intelligence testing has again moved into the limelight, yet the growth of a satisfactory theoretical basis, generally agreed upon by psychologists, has advanced hardly at all since the testing of 1917" (1941, p. 592). Although much that he discussed during this talk has been lost to posterity (only an abstract of his paper was later published), he appears to have highlighted several reasons for his dissatisfaction with the Binet-inspired tests of his day, and also with the prevailing unitary theories of intelligence. In general, he found both the testing and theory to lack applicability to adult populations, given that most assessments up to that point were child focused, and therefore so were the theories based on research using those assessments. From this unpublished talk grew a line of theory and research that has remained enormously influential for nearly 75 years.

In a series of studies and books, both on his own (e.g., 1941, 1963, 1967, 1971, 1987) and in collaboration with John Horn

(Horn & Cattell, 1966a, 1966b, 1967), Cattell developed a two-factor theory of intelligence. This model consists of fluid intelligence (*Gf*), which encompasses the ability to think and act quickly, solve novel problems, and encode short-term memories; and crystallized intelligence (*Gc*), the breadth and depth of a person's accumulated knowledge of a culture and the ability to use that knowledge to solve problems, use of language (vocabulary), and a wide variety of acquired skills. Horn went on to produce a number of seminal papers on the theory (1967, 1976), and today this theoretical approach is often referred to as the Cattell–Horn theory.

Fluid intelligence is relatively independent of education and acculturation but subject to physiological influences; crystallized intelligence emerges from learning and acculturation, with personality, motivation, and educational and cultural opportunity fostering its development.

Given that one motivation for the theory was Cattell's dissatisfaction with models that did not take human life-span development into account, it is not surprising that a great deal of longitudinal and cross-sectional research has been conducted on fluid and crystallized abilities. In general, these studies provide evidence that fluid intelligence peaks in early adulthood and then steadily declines as people age, most likely due to a loss of cognitive capacity to solve complex problems (Horn, Donaldson, & Engstrom, 1981). In contrast, crystallized intelligence appears to remain stable or increase throughout adulthood (see Hertzog & Schaie, 1986; Horn, 1970, 1998; Horn & Cattell, 1967; Horn & Donaldson, 1976; McArdle, Hamagami, Meredith, & Bradway, 2000). However, McArdle, Ferrer-Caja, Hamagami, and Woodcock (2002) found slightly different results: *Gf* and *Gc* both decline after an early adulthood peak, but the rate of increase slows more rapidly for *Gf* before the peak, and the rate of decline is faster after the peak.

Horn's most recent work, done primarily with Hiromi Masanga, suggests that in adulthood people funnel their abilities into areas of expertise. This decreases the use and, therefore, the retention of fluid abilities, but creates in the areas of expertise a kind of wide-span memory that enables the person to bring large amounts of information into immediate memory and use. Ericsson and Kintsch (1995) first noticed this, but Masanaga and Horn have made it part of extended *Gf-Gc* theory. Also important is adult expertise reasoning. It enables experts, such as adults in major positions of responsibility in our culture, to reason at a higher level than people who depend primarily on fluid reasoning. This part of the theory is most important for understanding why so much of our culture—our technology as well as our business and political practices—is in the hands of adults aged well over age 40 and extending into the 60s and 70s. Psychologist Paul Baltes integrated this idea into his "selective optimization with compensation" theory of human development. As people age they can learn to optimize their crystallized abilities or use them to compensate for age-related losses in fluid intelligence. For example, an aging chess master may find that he is no longer at the top of his game in speed chess. He could choose to compensate by playing speed chess only with other senior citizens, or to selectively optimize by focusing instead on traditional chess. The chess master's expertise in this domain (crystallized abilities) will continue to be an advantage when he competes against less-experienced players who may hold advantages in fluid intelligence (Baltes & Carstensen, 1996).

A distinct yet related perspective was offered by John Carroll, whose book *Human Cognitive Abilities* (1993) analyzed data from a few hundred previous studies in an attempt to build on the work of Thurstone, Guilford, Horn and Cattell, and Wechsler (Carroll, 1997). Based on his analyses, he proposed a three-level model of intelligence. Stratum I includes dozens of "narrow" abilities, such as quantitative reasoning, verbal language comprehension, memory span, memory for sound patterns, perceptual speed, and simple reaction time. These abilities each correspond to one of eight broad areas that constitute Stratum II, including fluid intelligence, crystallized intelligence, general memory and learning, broad visual perception, broad auditory perception, broad retrieval ability, broad cognitive speediness, and processing speed. Stratum III is a general hierarchical factor similar to g.

Carroll (1997) emphasized that his model has a number of advantages over previous efforts, including that it "directs attention to many types of ability usually ignored in traditional paradigms" and "implies that individual profiles of ability levels are much more complex than previously thought," all while offering a framework for understanding the complex organization of human cognitive ability (p. 128). In a major replication of Carroll's model, Bickley, Keith, and Wolfle (1995) largely replicated the proposed model and found that it was relatively stable across the life span.

There has been some dispute about whether the Gf-Gc theory or three-stratum theory better explains the results of some popular intelligence tests (e.g., Cole & Randall, 2003), in part because Horn and Carroll disagreed fairly sharply about the existence of a single, overarching factor.[5] These debates, however, have been overshadowed by McGrew's (1997) combination of three-stratum theory with Gf-Gc theory (hence the name Cattell–Horn–Carroll or CHC theory). He identified broad Stratum II factors that largely address discrepancies between the CHC approaches: fluid intelligence/reasoning, quantitative reasoning/knowledge, crystallized intelligence/knowledge, short-term memory, visual intelligence/processing, auditory intelligence/processing, long-term associative storage and retrieval, cognitive processing speed, decision/reaction time or speed, and reading/writing. CHC theory is especially influential within the field of school psychology, with its heavy emphasis on the use of cognitive assessments, and the theory has held up well in subsequent research (see Keith & Reynolds, 2010; Taub & McGrew, 2004; Willis, Dumont, & Kaufman, 2011).

AND NOW FOR SOMETHING COMPLETELY DIFFERENT

The common theme running through the theories presented so far in this chapter—and, for that matter, through nearly all the theories up to this point in the book—is that they were either derived from or primarily influenced by testing. In the early 1980s the field experienced a sea change in how intelligence was viewed. A major theme in this new class of ideas was a strong theoretical base and a less central role for testing. This is not to suggest that testing is not relevant to these approaches or that earlier theories were not conceptually strong. But, as you will see, the new theories have a very different feel than the earlier work.

The Theory of Multiple Intelligences

Howard Gardner, a well-known developmental psychologist, arrived at his theory from a very different perspective compared with many of the psychologists who preceded him: "My approach to the study of intelligence was unusual, if not unique, in that it minimized the importance of tests and of correlations among test scores. Rather, I proceeded from a definition and set of criteria" (Gardner, 1999, p. 113). As part of a large collaborative project begun in the late 1970s, Gardner endeavored to examine human potential, and in 1983 he published his seminal book, *Frames of Mind*, which has been released in new editions in 1993 and 2003.

Gardner defines intelligence as "the ability to solve problems or to fashion products that are valued in at least one culture or community" (1999, p. 113), and in Chapter 4 of *Frames of Mind* he lists several criteria for inclusion of an intelligence in his model, although he hastens to add that the prospect of meeting all of the criteria perfectly is probably not realistic. The criteria include potential isolation by brain damage, given that individuals with localized brain damage often demonstrate severe deficits that are circumscribed to a single cognitive domain; the existence of individuals with exceptional but uneven profiles of abilities, such as savants and prodigies; identifiable core information-processing mechanisms that correspond to a particular intelligence; distinct developmental pathways along with definable "end-states," such as being able to identify both novices and experts within a given domain; an evolutionary history suggesting that a particular intelligence has developed within humans over time or is present in lower life forms; experimental support; psychometric support; and encoding in a symbol system (i.e., culturally derived sets of symbols that assist in communicating concepts, such as language, mathematics, and musical notation).[6]

This approach stands in obvious sharp contrast to those of Galton, Goddard, and Spearman, but it also differs considerably from other approaches, such as Thurstone's, that laid out criteria before sifting through the data. And one need only browse the end notes in *Frames of Mind* for conclusive proof that multiple intelligences (MI) theory comes from a very different place than most previous conceptualizations of intelligence; for example, in addition to noting the work of Galton, Spearman, Thurstone, and other usual suspects, Gardner discusses the work of numerous philosophers, cognitive scientists studying both humans and nonhuman animals, communication researchers, mathematicians, linguists, acting teachers, and musicians, among many other "unusual suspects."[7]

At this point, it is important to once again consider the historical context in which this work was being conducted. The situated nature of cognition and learning—the fact that processes such as learning happen in specific social, cultural, and physical contexts—was receiving more attention within the social sciences than in the past, and Gardner, as someone who was leading the charge in his study of artistic development, traumatic brain injuries, and other topics, not surprisingly brought this highly contextualized perspective into his study of human ability and intelligence.

The initial seven intelligences proposed by Gardner are linguistic, logical-mathematical, spatial, bodily-kinesthetic, musical, interpersonal, and intrapersonal. Linguistic intelligence represents the ability to read, write, and speak well. Logical-mathematical intelligence encompasses logical thinking (e.g., chess strategy, deductive reasoning) as well as mathematical and scientific problem solving. Spatial intelligence is manifest when an individual navigates an unfamiliar set of streets, or when an architect visualizes plans for a building. Musical intelligence generates the set of skills that allow musicians to play a tune by ear, or to execute a phrase with sensitivity and grace. Bodily-kinesthetic intelligence is necessary for problem solving that requires use of the physical body, as is necessary for performing a complex surgical procedure, executing a series of dance steps, or catching a fly ball. Interpersonal intelligence is manifest in one's social skills, empathy, and intuition about what motivates other people. Intrapersonal intelligence involves a similar set of abilities turned toward oneself, leading to self-understanding.

Gardner claims that logical-mathematical and linguistic intelligences are overemphasized in traditional models of human intelligence, but he posits that this overemphasis is largely a cultural artifact; given different life circumstances, different intelligences would gain higher priority (Gardner, 1993). This hypothesis seems to be reflected in the works of scholars such as Diamond (1999).

Since his initial proposal of the seven intelligences, Gardner has added two candidates, naturalist and existential, while largely dismissing the idea of spiritual intelligence (Gardner, 1999, 2006). Individuals with high naturalist intelligence have the ability to identify and classify patterns in nature, and often show unusual interest in the natural world early in life. People who possess high existential intelligence are better able than most to make sense out of the "ultimate" concerns of human beings, such as the meaning of life and death, or the puzzle of the existence of single individuals in a vast and empty universe. Although Gardner proffers this final category of intelligence very cautiously, the limited evidence that has been gleaned suggests that it meets the same empirical criteria as the original seven. He has also carefully considered the idea of spiritual intelligence, which has often been recommended to him over the years, but he apparently believes that it fails to meet enough of the criteria to justify its inclusion in the model.

Gardner's work has been especially well received within educational circles. This book's first author vividly remembers walking into one of the country's top architecture schools in the early 1990s and, after some faculty recognized his interest in intelligence, being engaged in lengthy conversations about the applicability of MI theory to architecture and training architects (the faculty did most of the talking!). Much of the allure of MI theory may be that it formalizes what most people, notably teachers, want to believe about human beings: We are each unique, and we each have the potential to be excellent in one or more specific areas. We cautiously note that this popular interpretation of MI theory almost certainly is not shared by Gardner. But in our experience, this is how it is often viewed.

MI theory has received its fair share of stinging criticism, as one would expect for an approach that differs so markedly from efforts in the past. Some of this criticism stems from the criteria of psychometric support mentioned earlier. Some of the proposed intelligences do not easily lend themselves to assessment, and there are methodological issues with many traditional assessments that tend to bias results against support for MI theory. For example, note the conflicting results of recent attempts to assess the intelligences, as exemplified by Almeida et al. (2010); Castejon, Perez, and Gilar (2010); and Visser, Ashton, and Vernon (2006). Some critics have suggested that the intelligences are better conceptualized as talents or abilities. Jensen (1998), in a wide-ranging critique, finds the eight criteria to be too vague or "elastic," and he believes that many of the intelligences as currently described are not sufficiently distinguishable from g in experimental and psychometric settings (p. 129).

Gardner, to his credit, has publicly responded to the criticisms on multiple occasions (see, e.g., Gardner, 1995, 2006), but it is probably safe to conclude that fans of traditional psychometrics find MI theory to be severely wanting, whereas fans of culturally derived, contextualized developmental theory find a lot to like in MI theory.

Anecdotal evidence suggests that the theory has been enormously influential in changing educators' conceptions of intelligence and giftedness, widening the possibilities for which students are considered to be smart and talented. Although application of the theory to educational settings and interventions hasn't been without difficulties (e.g., Gardner, 1995; Plucker, 2000; Plucker, Callahan, & Tomchin, 1996; Pyryt, 2000), Gardner deserves credit for helping to change the conversation about how intelligence can and should be defined and modeled.

Triarchic Theory

Around the same time that Gardner was beginning his study of intelligence, Robert Sternberg began his influential line of research. Sternberg (2011a), whose background is rooted more firmly in cognitive and information-processing research, shares in an autobiographical note that he had a lifelong interest in intelligence, but it was only when he became a professor at Yale that the ideas for which he would become widely known began to take the shape we are familiar with:

> In teaching some graduate students, I became aware that different students had different patterns of abilities. One . . . was very high in the analytical skills measured by intelligence tests. But others were strong in skills not assessed by such tests. "Barbara" showed exceptional creative skills, "Celia" exceptional practical skills.

By 1985, . . . I argued that intelligence comprises not one unitary ability (so-called "*g*"), but rather, three interrelated abilities— analytical, creative, and practical. As time went on, it became clear . . . the theory was inadequate because one's intelligence was not merely a weighted sum or average of the three abilities. Rather, I began to think in terms of "successful intelligence," or one's intelligence as applied effectively to one's life. . . . [I]ntelligent people figure out what they want to do with their life and find a path to the successful realization of their goals. They do so by capitalizing on their strengths and compensating for or correcting their weaknesses, through a combination of analytical, creative, and practical abilities. (p. 310)

The triarchic theory of successful intelligence contends that these analytical, creative, and practical abilities function collectively to allow individuals to achieve success (Sternberg, 1988, 1996, 1999b). Analytical abilities enable the individual to evaluate, analyze, compare, and contrast information. Creative abilities generate invention, discovery, and other creative endeavors. Individuals use practical abilities to apply what they have learned in the appropriate settings, essentially serving to tie everything together.

Many of the ideas that are manifest in the theory of successful intelligence have been part of psychological discussions for generations. For example, Rudolf Pintner (1912/1969) defined intelligence as "the ability of the individual to adapt himself adequately to relatively new situations in life. It seems to include the capacity for getting along well in all sorts of situations. This implies ease and rapidity in making adjustments and, hence, ease in breaking old habits and in forming new ones" (p. 13). The value of Sternberg's work is in proposing—and evaluating and modifying—a theory based on a century of cognitive and social psychological research.

The theory also includes three subtheories: componential, experiential, and contextual. The componential subtheory addresses information-processing capabilities within the individual, with three specified mechanisms (the ability to learn, planning what to do, and carrying out the specified action). The experiential subtheory emphasizes the role of both novelty and automaticity as they relate to the individual's use of intelligence. The contextual subtheory focuses on the individual's ability to shape, adapt, and select his or her environment. These three subtheories provide a contextual perspective on the nature of intelligence, and suggest alternative approaches to the design of intelligence tests. According to Sternberg, traditional intelligence tests are limited by their overemphasis on facets of the componential subtheory, largely neglecting the other two (Sternberg, 1984). Sternberg and his colleagues have extensively studied applications of his work to educational contexts, with generally positive results (see Sternberg, 2011b, for a comprehensive review).

An important feature of Sternberg's theory, and this should not be a surprise given that his work was contemporaneous with Gardner's, is that the three intelligences operate within sociocultural contexts. To be successful in life individuals must make the best use of their analytical, creative, and practical strengths, while at the same time compensating for weaknesses in any of these areas. This might involve working on improving weak areas to become better adapted to the needs of a particular environment, or choosing to work in an environment that values the individual's particular strengths. For example, a person with highly developed analytical and practical abilities, but with less-developed creative abilities, might choose to work in a field that values technical expertise but does not require a great deal of imaginative thinking. Conversely, if the chosen career does value creative abilities, the individual can use his or her analytical strengths to come up with strategies for overcoming this weakness.

Thus, a central feature of the theory is adaptability, both within the individual and within the individual's sociocultural context (Cianciolo & Sternberg, 2004). But Sternberg (2011b) also cautions that intelligence "refers to more than 'adapting to the environment,' which is the mainstay of conventional definitions of intelligence. The theory . . . distinguishes among adapting, shaping, and selecting" (p. 505).

Indeed, Jensen (1998), in a generally favorable critique of the triarchic theory, states that it does not directly question the existence of g, and that many of Sternberg's components and subcomponents supplement g and are "really achievement variables that reflect how different individuals invest g in activities as affected by their particular opportunities, interests, personality traits, and motivation" (p. 133). Hunt (2011), in a less favorable review, raises these and additional issues and reviews (favorably) critiques of Sternberg's work by other scholars.

Sternberg (2011a) has responded to these and similar comments by noting, "I have gotten pushback from 'g' theorists and others who believe that my theories are too broad or even grandiose—from people who believe that general ability is the best predictor of success in most life endeavors and that other attributes are at the most part sideshows. They operate from a different metaphor of mind than I" (p. 312). Sternberg addresses this issue of "metaphors of mind" and makes the case that one's metaphorical approach to the study of intelligence says a lot about how he or she will view the available theories and evidence (1990). This is directly analogous to our theme throughout this book about the importance of understanding someone's definition of constructs, and also the historical and cultural context in which that person's work was conducted. The human mind is an amazing creativity engine, but it doesn't produce ideas or conduct research in a vacuum.

PASS Theory

Another very different approach to intelligence theory has been offered by J. P. Das, Jack Naglieri, and their colleagues, who have proposed the planning, attention-arousal, simultaneous, and successive (PASS) model of processing (Das, Kirby, & Jarman, 1975; Das, Naglieri, & Kirby, 1994). PASS is based on the work of Russian neuropsychologist A. R. Luria (1973), who proposed a three-unit model of human cognition: neurological arousal and attention (attention-arousal), simultaneous and successive information coding processes (simultaneous and successive), and the systemic use of information to inform behavior (planning).[8] (See Naglieri & Das, 2002, for a richer description.)

PASS theory challenges g theory on the grounds that neuropsychological research has demonstrated that the brain is made up of interdependent, but separate, functional systems. Neuroimaging studies and clinical studies of individuals with brain lesions provide evidence that the brain is modularized; for example, damage to a very specific area of the left temporal lobe will impair the production, but not the comprehension, of spoken and written language (a point also made by Gardner in his work with patients with brain injuries). Damage to an adjacent area will have the opposite impact, preserving the individual's ability to produce, but not understand, speech and text.

As implied above, PASS theory divides intelligence into four interrelated cognitive processes: planning, attention, simultaneous processing, and successive processing. Planning is the ability to make decisions about how to solve problems and perform actions. It involves setting goals, anticipating consequences, and using feedback. Planning also involves the attention and the simultaneous and successive processing functions, described below, and is associated with the frontal lobes of the brain. Attention involves the ability to selectively attend to stimuli while ignoring other distractions, and the higher attentional processes are thought to be related to the planning functions of the frontal lobe.

Simultaneous processing involves the ability to integrate separate stimuli into a cohesive, interrelated whole. Simultaneous processing is necessary for language comprehension, as in

"Bill is taller than Sue, but Mary is taller than Bill. Who is the tallest?" (Das et al., 1994, p. 72). The occipital and parietal lobes are thought to be important for these functions. Finally, successive processing involves the ability to integrate stimuli into a sequential order. An example of this process is the sequencing of letters and words in reading and writing. This type of processing is believed to be related to frontal-temporal lobe functioning (Das, 2002).

According to the PASS theory, information arrives at the senses from external and internal sources, at which point the four cognitive processes activate to analyze its meaning within the context of the individual's knowledge base (semantic and episodic knowledge, implicit and procedural memories, and so on). Thus, the same information can be processed in multiple ways (Das, 2002).

Interestingly, PASS doesn't receive as much attention—either expressions of support or criticisms—as one might expect. It is the theory underlying two popular intelligence assessments: the Cognitive Assessment System (Naglieri & Das, 1997) and the second edition of the Kaufman Assessment Battery for Children (Kaufman & Kaufman, 2004). However, it has received little attention in major reviews of intelligence theory and research. The research support is at least promising (Naglieri & Otero, 2011), leading us to conclude that it is "underweighted" in such discussions.

AND NOW FOR SOMETHING *REALLY* COMPLETELY DIFFERENT

One conceptualization of intelligence that we haven't yet covered is emotional intelligence (EI). Part of our struggle is figuring out where to put it. In the final chapter, framed as a promising new direction? That wouldn't work too well, as development of this area is more advanced than people realize. So then why not as a "new conception" in this chapter? That's not a great solution either, as EI theory and research are often quite different from the cognitively flavored conceptualizations discussed earlier. In the end, we decided to place it right here (for reasons that should become apparent), although we realize this transition is a little awkward.[9] We also chose not to provide an exhaustive overview of EI, because such a review would be lengthy; very good resources of that nature are already available (e.g., Matthews, Zeidner, & Roberts, 2012); and critiques of EI conceptualization, research, and application appear regularly (e.g., Cherniss, Extein, Goleman, & Weissberg, 2006; Ciarrochi, Chan, & Caputi, 2000; Joseph & Newman, 2010; Matthews et al., 2012; Waterhouse, 2006).

EI theory and research generally fall into three broad categories: ability conceptions, trait conceptions, and mixed approaches. The best-known ability conceptualization has been developed by Jack Mayer and Peter Salovey, who define the construct as "an ability to recognize the meanings of emotions and their relationships, and to reason and problem-solve on the basis of them. Emotional intelligence is involved in the capacity to perceive emotions, assimilate emotion-related findings, understand the information of those emotions, and manage them" (Mayer, Caruso, & Salovey, 2000, p. 267). In other words, EI is a distinct cognitive ability.

The Mayer–Salovey model has four components: reflectively regulating emotions, understanding emotions, assimilating emotion in thought, and perceiving and expressing emotion (Mayer & Salovey, 1997; Mayer et al., 2000). Interestingly, the four sets of skills are considered to be on a continuum, from lower-level (perception and expression of emotion) to higher-level (reflective regulation of emotion) skills. It's easy to perceive the cognitive flavor of the Mayer–Salovey model, as it is to see why they believe such skills can be measured and taught. In addition, their work feels similar to MI theory in many ways, and also to parts of triarchic theory that emphasize contextual understanding to apply cognitive skills.

Trait models, which Cherniss (2010) has described as "second generation model[s]" (p. 112) because they build on the first wave of ability and mixed models, are designed to include personality characteristics that deal with affect. In the words of Matthews et al. (2012), a trait conception of EI "refers to typical behaviors and ways of experiencing the world, rather than a true ability" (p. 43). Perhaps the best-known work is this area has been conducted by K. V. Petrides and colleagues, who have essentially posited a hierarchical model of trait EI that includes higher-order factors of emotionality, self-control, sociability, and well-being (Petrides, 2011; Petrides & Furnham, 2003; Petrides, Furnham, & Mavroveli, 2007). Research using instruments specifically designed to assess trait EI has largely supported this model and its relationship to important socioemotional outcomes (e.g., Frederickson, Petrides, & Simmonds, 2012; see Matthews et al., 2012, for a thorough review).

Mixed models have characteristics of both the ability and trait approaches, with the work of Bar-On (1997, 2000, 2005) being the most prominent and influential. Bar-On's conceptualization includes 5 higher-order factors (i.e., intrapersonal, interpersonal, stress management, adaptability, and general mood) and 15 lower-order dimensions. Using measures based specifically on this model, Bar-On and colleagues have found relationships between "EQ" and several indicators of well-being and success, such as job performance (e.g., Bar-On, Handley, & Fund, 2005). Although mixed models are dealt a great deal of criticism in the literature, their early contributions to the study of EI need to be acknowledged.

All of this theory and research prompts an important question: Is EI really a form of intelligence? Wechsler (1940), for example, argued that "non-intellective" factors such as personality are influential in the development of intelligence, acknowledging the importance of these factors but distinguishing them from intelligence. Mayer et al. (2000) have directly addressed this issue, proposing three criteria for a construct to be labeled an "intelligence." Simplified somewhat, their criteria are:

1. *Conceptual:* An intelligence must represent "mental performance" rather than nonintellectual constructs such as self-concept or "preferred ways of behaving."
2. *Correlational:* An intelligence should be empirically distinct from other, "already established" conceptions of intelligence, and it should consist of abilities that are closely related (i.e., it should be both internally consistent and externally distinct).
3. *Developmental:* An intelligence should change as people age and gain experience in relevant areas.

Based on these criteria, Mayer, Salovey, and their colleagues believe that their ability conception of EI is, in fact, a distinct intelligence. But they do not make the claim that other models meet these criteria. In fact, they take a pretty dim view of those other approaches:

> Emotional intelligence has often been conceptualized (particularly in popular literature) as involving much more than ability at perceiving, assimilating, understanding, and managing emotions. These alternative conceptions include not only emotion and intelligence per se, but also motivation, non-ability dispositions and traits, and global personal and social functioning. . . . Such broadening seems to undercut the utility of the terms under consideration. . . . [These "mixed" models] must be analyzed carefully so as to distinguish the concepts that are a part of emotional

intelligence from the concepts that are mixed in, or confounded, with it. (Mayer et al., 2000, p. 268)

We tend to view ability-focused models as most closely conforming to what people usually mean when they talk about intelligence, with personality trait models being aspects of personality and affect rather than intelligence. That's not to say the trait and mixed models are not valuable and important; it simply feels like a stretch to label them different forms of intelligence.

SO . . . WHERE ARE WE WITH ALL THIS?

Much has been made of the lack of empirical support for contemporary conceptualizations of intelligence. Critics often go so far as to question whether these "theories" are merely wishful thinking by scholars who are unhappy with classic, psychometric approaches such as g but are unable to create a suitable alternative.

These critics are somewhat selective in that they overlook inconvenient evidence, and they strike us as a bit impatient, since researchers have had a century to gather support for g and contemporary researchers have had much less time. Some of the criticisms are somewhat amusing from a historical perspective, such as knocking Gardner for telling people what they want to hear . . . just as Galton was criticized nearly a century and a half earlier.

At the same time, strong empirical support for some of the contemporary theories is not accumulating at the pace one would expect. However, in balance, the breadth of contemporary theory should be seen as a positive development: Historically, researchers dissatisfied with psychometric conceptualizations had few alternatives; contemporary theories have their weaknesses, but their conceptual and methodological breadth is refreshing.

One frustrating thing about the debates is the extent to which the various parties are talking past one another. This disconnect is due largely to, as Sternberg puts it, each party using a different "metaphor of mind"; put in terms we have used in this book, each side is operationalizing its constructs differently. Many researchers are very happy with the current conceptualization of g and see contemporary theories as overreaching; many contemporary theorists believe that application to real contexts is a form of theoretical validity that their theories address better than g. The difference, we suspect, is largely a matter of definition.

ARE YOU FULL OF MULTIPOTENTIALITY?

What do all these theories mean? Do all the differences really matter? Those are fair questions, and we are tempted to address them with a ton of examples. However, we don't want you to fall asleep, so we will provide just one example of why these differences matter: the debate over the existence of multipotentiality, the idea that a person can have high levels of potential to excel in several different areas. From a counseling perspective, the areas are construed broadly: Can someone have potential in writing, science, and dance? From a research perspective, the argument tends to be limited to traditional academic and cognitive areas: Can someone have potential in writing, chemistry, mathematics, and history?

If multipotentiality exists, it can lead to several problems for a talented person, including difficulty narrowing career options, outside pressure to pursue high-status (or high-income) careers, the necessity to make long-term commitments to education and training (e.g., graduate or professional school) even in the face of confusion about career path or decisions related to other priorities (e.g., starting a family), and perfectionist tendencies (e.g., looking for the "perfect" career) (Rysiew, Shore, & Leeb, 1999). If multipotentiality doesn't exist, then counseling strategies designed to assist students as they consider multiple career paths may be targeted incorrectly. In other words, if your talent lies in chemistry, waiting too long to choose a career because you want to leave your options open may actually limit your chances of success in the long run.

The research base is rather mixed, with some studies supporting (Gagné, 1998; Kerr & Erb, 1991) and others harshly criticizing (Achter, Benbow, & Lubinski, 1996; Legree, Pifer, & Grafton, 1996; Milgram & Hong, 1999) the idea of multipotentiality. One of our favorite quotes in this debate is by Robinson (1997), who noted that ceiling effects on tests may falsely give the appearance of multipotentiality (i.e., the high end of the test is too easy, so bright people all score in a clump at the 99th percentile). She notes that these effects need to be addressed, because their existence may actually be "maintaining an illusion of equal potentials across the board" (p. 217).

How would various intelligence theorists view multipotentiality? Proponents of unitary views would probably be sympathetic, since they generally believe that many of the core cognitive components of intelligence underlie intellectual work across domains. Holders of multiple views would probably vary more in their attitudes toward the idea of multiple potentials, which isn't surprising from a historical perspective: The era in which many of the differentiated theories were formed was also characterized by the principle that human activity is often—if not always—context dependent and situated in specific domains. As we've discussed throughout this book, every intelligence theory should be considered within its historical context, as the intellectual themes of the day are often intertwined in the theories that occur within those time periods.

So, once again, where one stands on the structure of intelligence largely colors how one views issues of multipotentiality. Where does this leave a practitioner, such as a guidance counselor who is trying to work with a bright high school student trying to prepare for college and career? In the end, gifted students and parents of talented students believe multipotentiality is a problem (Moon, Kelly, & Feldhusen, 1997), and arguing that it does not exist is probably not going to work well. At the same time, counselors should try to avoid the ceiling effects in testing noted by Robinson, so that more accurate profiles of student strengths can be examined.

WHAT DO YOU BELIEVE ABOUT YOUR OWN INTELLIGENCE?

Before we close this chapter, we want to introduce you to one more very important idea: What you believe about your own intelligence matters. A lot. Do you believe that your intelligence just "is what it is"—a fixed, unchangeable trait? Or do you believe that your intelligence is malleable and can be improved with effort? The way you answer this question may have profound implications for your future intellectual, academic, and career success. Here's why.

Decades of research from the American psychologist Carol Dweck and her colleagues demonstrates that people who believe that their intelligence is malleable are more willing to take on intellectual challenges than are people who believe that intelligence is a fixed internal characteristic. Equally important, people who believe they can improve their intelligence are more likely to persist at difficult tasks when the going gets rough (Deiner & Dweck, 1978, 1980; Dweck, 1975, 1999, 2007). This makes intuitive sense: If you believe that your intelligence is a fixed trait, you will probably place high value on the appearance of success. An A on a test is pretty good evidence that you are intelligent, right? However, if you believe that your intelligence is malleable, you might risk taking a harder class where you will learn more but earn a grade of B. This won't bother you that much because the harder class helped you to increase your intelligence.

This fundamental difference in attitude is often conceptualized as the difference between a performance orientation (appearing smart) and a mastery orientation (focusing on the actual learning). It turns out that the way students are praised plays a major role in determining whether a person develops the healthy mastery orientation or the somewhat neurotic performance orientation. Praising students for being intelligent when they succeed may seem to be a good idea, but it really isn't. Take, for example, the case of a student who gets 100% on her math test. A teacher or parent may choose to praise her by saying something like "You're so smart at math!" This sends the message that success is evidence of intelligence. In this case, how willing will that student be to take on intellectual challenges that carry some risk of failure? After all, it is much less risky to take the safe route and get that easy A. The teacher or parent would do better to praise for effort instead: "You worked so hard on that math homework, and it really paid off!" This teaches the student that intelligence can be increased through effort and persistence, setting the stage for a mastery orientation and an increased potential for maximum intellectual growth.[10]

TAKEAWAYS

- Unitary conceptions maintain a following of researchers and theorists, and should not be discounted as a major influence on the contemporary study of intelligence.

- Over time, theories have broadened to include multifaceted, often hierarchical models of intelligence.
- Psychometrically derived theories generally favor the existence of a unitary intelligence, although the Horn–Cattell and Carroll models do not agree on this point.
- Theories of intelligence tend to reflect the historical and cultural contexts within which they are created.
- Multipotentiality may or may not exist, but ceiling effects in testing definitely are real and should be considered when one is looking at data about a particular person's abilities and potential for future success.

NOTES

1. Who says students can't make major contributions?
2. Essentially, don't go into a study looking for g; go into a study looking for what the data tell you.
3. For example, he refined the IQ score to reflect score distributions, essentially replacing the mental age approach to calculating IQ scores, which was widely used at the time.
4. Apologies to Crosby, Stills, Nash, and Sometimes Young.
5. As you would imagine, Horn, no; Carroll, yes.
6. See Chapter 4 of Gardner (1983) for a more detailed overview of these criteria.
7. When someone references the work of Noam Chomsky, Thornton Wilder, Jean-Paul Sartre, and Igor Stravinsky in the same chapter, it's a safe bet that you're reading a different perspective on human intelligence!
8. We thought the same thing you're thinking now, but A-ASSP isn't a great acronym. Also, although Das uses the term attention-arousal, Naglieri focuses more on attention, and we use his nomenclature from this point forward, as he has applied PASS theory to assessment more than any other researcher.

9. If you're bothered by this, perhaps you should develop more EI.

10. There are other, well-developed lines of research on people's beliefs about intelligence, including work on "implicit theories" (i.e., people's personal theories), especially on how these beliefs differ developmentally or across cultures (e.g., Berg & Sternberg, 1985; Grigorenko et al., 2001; Lim, Plucker, & Im, 2002). This work is important and interesting, but it is a bit off topic here.

Nature or Nurture? What the Flynn Effect Tells Us About Intelligence

The origins of intelligence have been hotly debated since the construct was first studied. In an earlier chapter we described the beginnings of the eugenics movement in the United States and the societal concerns of Goddard, who was convinced that intelligence was primarily a matter of hereditary endowment and worried that allowing individuals with low intelligence to breed unchecked would result in a gradual decrease in U.S. national intelligence (Goddard, 1912b, 1914, 1917). Goddard's concerns were mirrored by Galton, who approached the same issue from the inverse perspective: Individuals with exceptional intellectual gifts should be encouraged to interbreed in order to gradually increase the number of living "geniuses" (Galton, 1884b). Goddard's and Galton's warnings notwithstanding, human intelligence has apparently been steadily increasing in the United States, Great Britain, and many other nations (e.g., Flynn, 1984, 1998, 2010). So there is a reasonable chance that you may actually be "smarter" than your parents, at least in some ways. But you already knew that, right?

This finding was reported for the first time in 1984 by James Flynn, who found that people living in the United States were gaining a little more than 3 points per decade on tests of human intelligence.[1] This equated to an increase in mean IQ score of 13.8 points—nearly one standard deviation—over the 46-year span of his initial investigation (Flynn, 1984). These IQ gains over time have been given the eponymous name the Flynn effect, which we will abbreviate here as the FE. The comment that you might be "smarter" than your parents is obviously our attempt at humor, but the FE is actually a profoundly serious matter. It has sparked considerable interest and controversy among contemporary scholars of human intelligence, and, as you will see later, arguments about the FE have had, and will continue to have, life-and-death consequences for some individuals (see Flynn, 2006, 2007, 2009; Kaufman, 2009, 2010).

To understand the FE, it is important to understand that an IQ is not an absolute score, but rather a relative score that provides information about a person's performance in comparison with other individuals of the same age who took an IQ test. IQs are carefully calibrated to fit the normal curve, with a mean (arbitrarily chosen based on historical conventions) of 100 and (often) a standard deviation of 15. Using the normal curve, it is easy to take any IQ score and see what percentage of a given population would be expected to score above or below it. Some scores, such as those below 70 or above 130, are very rare (a little more than 2% of the population each) and can be used to make decisions about whether or not a particular person is intellectually handicapped (below 70) or gifted (above 130) (Kaufman, 2009).

For this to work, potential IQ tests must be standardized ("normed") based on a representative sample of the population as it exists at the time the tests are being normed. This means that a very large sample of people of various ages approximating the ethnic, socioeconomic, and geographical makeup of the overall population must answer the questions that are being vetted for a potential IQ test, so that the test developers know approximately how many people of each age in a population are likely to answer each particular question correctly. Once this elaborate and time-consuming process is complete, the test can be published and used by clinicians and researchers. In the past, test developers normed tests very infrequently: There was a gap of 25 years between the Wechsler Intelligence Scale for Children (WISC; Wechsler, 1949) and the WISC-R (Wechsler, 1974), and it was another 17 years before the WISC-III was published (Wechsler, 1991). However, since Flynn discovered that people tend to score higher on older tests of intelligence, IQ test developers have been careful to re-norm IQ tests with greater regularity (Kaufman, 2009, 2010).[2]

Flynn's methods were relatively straightforward. He collected every study he could locate in which two or more intelligence tests had been administered to the same set of individuals. The studies chosen were limited to those that used tests that had been normed more than 6 years apart (providing at least one "old" test and one newer one). To maximize validity, Flynn applied various exclusion criteria. For example, studies were eliminated from the investigation if there was a substantial danger of practice effects due to large carryover of content from one test to another, if the interval between test administrations was 2 or more years (suggesting that actual IQ may have changed in the interim between the two test administrations), if the subjects taking the test experienced a dramatic life change (such as changing from an enriched school to an impoverished one) between test administrations, or if the data from the study did not include the full range of IQ as depicted by the normal curve. Seventy-three studies including data from nearly 7,500 test subjects remained, reflecting information from 18 combinations of tests across eight standardization samples.

Flynn used standardization data from each test version to create a uniform scoring convention for computing the mean scores for each test administered. His findings showed that, in general, examinees performed substantially better on the older tests, indicating that the older norm groups were not as "smart" as the newer norm groups they were compared against. These IQ gains were consistent across all age groups examined (ages 2 to 48 years) and were approximately linear from 1932 to 1978. The linear pattern suggests that people were getting smarter at a relatively consistent rate over time.

In 1987 Flynn published the results of a follow-up study showing test data from 14 nations revealing similar gains ranging between 5 and 25 IQ points in a single generation (Flynn, 1987). This time, however, he focused closely on the much higher gains in subtests and tests that purported to measure fluid rather than crystallized intelligence (Kaufman, 2009, 2010). Enormous gains in the WISC Similarities subtest—largely a fluid measure—and the Raven's Progressive Matrices test (1981)—also assumed to measure fluid intelligence—were particularly notable. Fluid intelligence is believed to be less dependent on formal learning and life experience, so these results were surprising (Ceci & Kanaya, 2010). They showed that the FE could not be explained by generational improvements in exposure to an ever-growing knowledge base. People were not just knowing more. They were knowing *differently*. Their abilities to solve novel problems logically and to think abstractly were improving faster than their knowledge of items such as information or vocabulary (Flynn, 2007).

At the time of this writing, the FE has been found in 29 countries (Ceci & Kanaya, 2010; see also Flynn, 1998, 1999, 2007, 2009; Wechsler, 1991; Zhou, Zhu, & Weiss, 2010). In most countries the trend of gains in IQ has continued throughout the 20th and into the 21st century (e.g., Ceci & Kanaya, 2010; Flynn, 2007; Flynn & Weiss, 2007; Kaufman 2009; Zhou & Zhu, 2007). However, it appears to have halted or begun to reverse in Norway (Sundet, Barlaug, & Torjussen, 2004) and Denmark (Teasdale & Owen, 2005, 2008). Yang, Zhu, Pinon, and Wilkins (2006) reported that the FE is now reversing in the United States for very young children. A study of nearly 2 million test scores provided by fifth-, sixth-, and seventh-grade students in the United States demonstrates that the FE remains robust among high-ability (top 5%) youth (Wai & Putallaz, 2011).

CAUSES OF THE FLYNN EFFECT

The consensus among scholars is that the rise in the global IQ score seen internationally is real (McGrew, 2010). However, considerable controversy surrounds its causes (Ceci & Kanaya, 2010). Researchers have put forward a variety of explanations, including improvements in nutrition (Colom, Lluis-Font, & Andres-Pueyo, 2005), advances in public health (Steen, 2009), better education (Teasdale & Owen, 2005), the environment in general (Dickens & Flynn, 2001), and, rarely, genetics (Rodgers & Wanstrom, 2007). A few researchers have suggested that the FE might be nothing more than a statistical or methodological artifact (Beaujean & Osterlind, 2008; Rodgers, 1998).

The substantially greater gains in fluid versus crystallized intelligence led Flynn to conclude that the FE was caused by a societal shift from concrete to abstract thinking. He concluded that the rise of scientific technology has encouraged more recent generations to solve problems using abstract rather than concrete approaches. These "new habits of mind" privilege detached logic and hypothetical reasoning, and may reflect a dramatic change from the kind of processing used by prior generations (Flynn, 2007, p. 53). In past generations,

> intelligence was anchored in everyday reality. We differ from them in that we can use abstractions . . . to attack the formal problems that arise when science liberates thought from concrete situations. Since 1950, we have become more ingenious . . . to solve problems on the spot. (Flynn, 2007, pp. 10–11)

Robert Sternberg believes that Flynn's explanation is plausible. However, he has suggested that the rise in scientific technology and thinking cannot account for the uniform rise in IQ in many nations of the world because technological innovation and educational availability and quality are anything but uniform. It is more likely that multiple, interacting causes account for the FE, notably "the increased complexity of the world and the increase in intelligence needed to adapt successfully to this world" (Sternberg, 2010, p. 435). He likens the world to a "global parent that directs people to develop certain skills over others, such as abstract thinking and symbolic reasoning of the kinds measured by IQ tests. . . . Skills develop in part as a reflection of the demands of the environment: Abstract reasoning has become more important in today's world" (2010, p. 436).

Alan Kaufman (2010) has also pointed out several potential flaws in Flynn's argument. He acknowledges the existence of the FE and its magnitude in terms of global IQ scores. He is very critical, however, of Flynn's (2007, 2009) explanation of generational gains in particular IQ subtest scores as measures of generational gains in the capacity for abstract thinking. At issue are the substantial changes made in test content, administration procedures, and scoring guidelines when the WISC (Wechsler, 1949) was revised to become the WISC-R (Wechsler, 1974). The changes meant that when Flynn compared children's performance on the older and newer tests, he was comparing apples to oranges. Specifically, Flynn should not have anchored so many of his arguments about the rise in fluid intelligence on the massive gains on the Similarities subtest between the WISC and subsequent WISC revisions. "Much of that alleged gain," Kaufman explained, "is bogus" (Kaufman, 2010, p. 384). Following are some of the reasons why.

First, the revision of the 1949 WISC included a shift in age range for the test from 5–15 years to 6–16 years. This required some meaningful adjustments to item difficulty and type. Many of these substantial changes were made to the Similarities subtest and other subtests pertinent to FE interpretation (Kaufman, 1990, 2010). Second, the wording of some Similarities subtest questions was changed in the revised version to reflect new research findings indicating that some young or culturally disadvantaged children sometimes misunderstood the older wording, leading to lower subtest scores. Third, in the administration of the WISC, no feedback was provided to children to indicate that abstract answers were preferred over concrete ones, or that the speed with which they solved some items counted toward their score; this changed with the WISC-R. Finally, the WISC-R provided more explicit and clear directions to the examiner as to when and how to ask an examinee to clarify his or her response; this means that the WISC-R scores were probably more accurate reflections of the children's ability to think abstractly.

Kaufman also identified important changes to the Wechsler Adult Intelligence Scale (WAIS; Wechsler, 1955), noting that these changes were so important that "it is not possible to interpret gains on this task from 1947 to 1972, yet that is precisely what Flynn (2007) has done" (2010, p. 385). Since, for the most part, foreign versions of the WISC and WAIS closely mirror their U.S. counterparts (through close translations of items rather than through adaptations of item content to suit a particular cultural context), problems identified with the U.S. data apply internationally as well (see van de Vijver, Mylonas, Pavlopoulos, & Georgas, 2003).

Kaufman (2010) also attempted to defuse Flynn's (1999, 2007, 2009) arguments using data on substantial gains in scores on Raven's (1938, 2000) Progressive Matrices by noting that the types of items on Raven's test were totally unfamiliar to earlier generations of test takers, but that this is no longer the case. Books and websites containing similar items proliferate in the media, as a quick web search using "Raven's Matrices" will show. Raven's and Raven's-type items are now used diagnostically with considerable frequency, and often by nonpsychologists. That means that the items are not as closely guarded by professional and ethical constraints as are the items on the Wechsler tests (American Psychological Association, 2002), so that later generations of people can, and do, practice them. Thus, Kaufman raised the question of how much of the purported gain in fluid intelligence is actually due to test sophistication and practice effects.

In a rebuttal article, Flynn (2010) argued that his methodology accounted for the changes in the WISC and WAIS, and he disputed the easy availability of Raven's-type items in books and on the Internet (2010). His own search at bookstores revealed that most puzzle books contain very few, if any, items similar to the Raven's type. Moreover, he found many books containing items similar to the WISC Picture Completion, Information, and Vocabulary subtests. Consequently, if people are practicing, then they have the opportunity to practice for other IQ tests also, and the Raven's test should not be singled out for the purposes of this critique. He granted that test sophistication and practice effects may be issues because people are more familiar with puzzles in general, but this likely accounts for only about 25% of the gains in Raven's scores. If the impact of cumulative practice effect over time is set as a maximum of 6 points (as suggested by Jensen, 1980), the FE is reduced. Therefore, a practice effect could decrease, for example, the Dutch 18-year-olds' 21-point gain between 1952 and 1982 to 15 points (Flynn, 1987), or the British adults' gain of 27 points between 1942 and 1992 to 21 (Flynn, 1998). Even accounting for practice effects, the overall gain in IQ would still be enormous.

THE FLYNN EFFECT AND SPECIAL POPULATIONS

The FE is a complex and multifaceted phenomenon of inherent intellectual interest to psychologists and others who are intrigued by the human capacity for growth and change. FE research has moved beyond purely academic interest, however. The FE has special relevance to certain vulnerable populations, and its implications are carefully monitored and debated in legal circles. As Cecil Reynolds pointed out, the decision of whether or not to adjust observed IQ scores for the FE has become "a dire matter with implications we seldom encounter in psychology" (Kaufman & Weiss, 2010, p. 380). This section will review some of those potentially dire implications.

Students Receiving Special Education Services

The FE has particular relevance for schoolchildren who have been given a diagnosis that qualifies them for special education services (Ceci & Kanaya, 2010). Typically, special education students are given IQ tests at least every 3 years. The FE suggests that there are two problems with this scenario. First, if the same test norms are used every time, a child's IQ score will gradually increase over time, possibly meaning that he or she may test out of essential educational services. Alternatively, if newer norms are used during retesting, the child's IQ score is likely to drop, giving the false impression that the child is actually losing ground (Ceci & Kanaya, 2010). Hard evidence comes from a study by Kanaya, Scullin, and Ceci (2003), who found that when the WISC-R was replaced with the newer WISC-III, the number of children who were diagnosed with mental retardation nearly tripled. Of course, overdiagnosis of intellectual disability carries with it the burden of increased costs incurred by schools and the potential for social stigma that lasts well beyond the school years (Ceci & Kanaya, 2010; see also Mercer, 1973).

To minimize the impact of the FE, Flynn (2007) has suggested correcting for outdated test norms by deducting 0.30 point from the examinee's score for each year the norms are out of date. This adjustment, often referred to as the Flynn correction, is sanctioned by many clinicians, researchers, and legal authorities (see Kaufman, 2009; 2010) and has been endorsed by the American Association of Intellectual and Developmental Disabilities (AAIDD; Schalock et al., 2010).

Capital Offense Cases

Atkins v. Virginia (2002) stipulated that convicted defendants who are mentally retarded[3] cannot be executed, as this is a violation of the Eighth Amendment ban on cruel and unusual punishment. Therefore, the sentencing phase in many capital murder cases now hinges on whether or not to apply the Flynn correction formula to adjust observed IQ scores (Fletcher, Stuebing, & Hughes, 2010; Flynn, 2006; Kaufman, 2009; Kaufman & Weiss, 2010). Given the enormity of the stakes in capital murder cases, the FE is now regularly used as evidentiary support. Indeed, several court cases stipulate that the FE must be taken into consideration in determining a defendant's IQ (Flynn, 2007). Generally, the procedure for determining intellectual disability is a complex process that takes into account such things as clinical judgment, adaptive functioning, observed IQ scores, and measurement error. However, given that experts on opposing sides of legal cases often disagree about the meaningfulness of various sources of evidence, the determination in many court cases often comes down to (a) indications of poor adaptive functioning and (b) observed IQ scores of 70 to 75 (Flynn, 2006). When observed IQ scores are borderline, the FE can mean the difference between life in prison and the death penalty. Consider the case of a convicted criminal who has an observed IQ score of 73 on a test with 20-year-old norms. If the court is using the most stringent guideline of 70 as the cutoff point for intellectual disability, this individual may be executed. However, the FE suggests that this IQ score is actually 6 points over what this individual would have received if he were retested using up-to-date norms. Applying the Flynn correction yields a new score of 67, situating the defendant safely under the bar and thus saving the individual's life (Kaufman & Weiss, 2010).

Prominent psychologists are often called upon to give expert testimony regarding the application of the FE (see Flynn, 2006; Kaufman, 2009). Many argue that since it is not practically feasible to re-norm the tests every year, the Flynn correction should always be used to find the appropriate normative comparison group for a particular defendant. As Fletcher et al. (2010) put it, "we would not expect pediatricians to use a height/weight chart from another country or century to assess a child's percentile rank in height or weight" (p. 470). Not all experts agree with this analogy, however. Recent FE research has yielded new information that may make some people less enthusiastic about the use of the Flynn correction.

Zhou, Zhu, and Weiss's (2010) examination of the FE demonstrates that the magnitude of the FE differs depending on the ability level of the individual being tested. Therefore, applying the same Flynn correction (0.30 point per year that the norms are out of date) for all ability levels will systematically yield over- or underestimates of IQ. Unfortunately, the different statistical analyses applied by the study authors yielded contradictory results, so it could not be determined from this study whether the FE changes are greater for individuals with lower, average, or high observed IQs. More work needs to be done to answer that question. In the meantime, however, Flynn (2010) maintains that it is better to err on the side of safety and use the approximate rule of 0.30 point per year in capital murder cases, or in situations where an IQ score of 70 or below is needed to qualify for specific benefits, such as special education services.

Hagan, Drogin, and Guilmette (2010) disagree with these conclusions on the grounds that it is preferable to use the obtained IQ score and then address factors that might impact its validity, rather than to use the Flynn correction to alter an obtained IQ score itself. They make this argument because the magnitude of the FE is "a moving target" in the literature that may vary by age group, ability level, and specific test used (pp. 474–475). Since the precise magnitude of the FE for a given individual cannot be known, it is inappropriate to apply a general formula when correcting it. Reynolds, Niland, Wright, and Rosenn (2010, p. 270) counter this, however, by reminding us that "nearly all effects in psychology are based on aggregated data and groups and subsequent probability estimations from groups to individuals." The bottom line for these researchers is that "[n]o one's life should depend on when an IQ test was normed" (Reynolds et al., 2010, p. 480).

NATURE VIA NURTURE

What is more important to the area of a rectangle, its height or its width (see Meaney, 2001)? If you are having trouble with this question, let's try another: What is more important to human intelligence, nature or nurture? It may be that these two questions have the same answer. Read on to see why.

The debate over the possible causes and meaning of the FE is just one contemporary incarnation of a very old argument about the relative importance of nature and nurture in the development of human intelligence. In Chapter 1 you learned that the "nature versus nurture" debate is a very old one. Plato tried—unsuccessfully—to offer the definitive answer in a dialogue featuring Socrates. In subsequent epochs the debate has taken many forms. As you've already seen, early influential writers such as Goddard and Galton represent the hereditarian extreme. Support for this view was buttressed in the mid-20th century when the famous British psychologist Sir Cyril Burt (1883–1971) published a series of papers that purported to show extraordinarily high correlations for the IQ scores of identical twins who had been separated at birth—compelling evidence that the different environments the twins experienced had very little impact on their intellectual ability (e.g., Burt, 1966). This might have settled the issue, at least for a while, if it had not been for the American psychologist Leon Kamin (b. 1927) and other critics who were skeptical of Burt's methodology. Subsequent analyses, which are not without their critics, suggest the possibility that Burt fabricated his data (see Kamin, 1974) . . . or maybe he didn't (see Mackintosh, 1995).

Burt's data notwithstanding, twin studies, adoptive parent studies, and other tools of behavior genetics have offered a great deal of legitimate empirical support for the idea that intelligence is at least in part—perhaps a rather large part—a matter of genetic endowment. Heritability estimates for intellectual abilities (statistics that describe the proportion of the variance in a trait within a specific population that can be attributed to genetic endowments) generally fall between 40% and 60% in well-respected studies (see Mandelman & Grigorenko, 2011). This means that one way to become intelligent is to pick good parents.

Of course, genes aren't everything. Some early researchers, such as the behaviorist John B. Watson (1878–1958), took a resolutely environmental stance, championing the supremacy of the environment in shaping intellect. A famous quote by Watson illustrates this view:

> Give me a dozen healthy infants, well-formed, and my own specified world to bring them up in and I'll guarantee to take any one at random and train him to become any type of specialist I might select—doctor, lawyer, artist . . . regardless of his talents, penchants, tendencies, abilities, vocations, and race of his ancestors. (Watson, 1930, p. 82)

Few 21st-century scholars would endorse Watson's view,[4] but behavior genetics research does provide evidence to support the idea that environment plays an essential role in determining intelligence. For example, various studies have shown IQ score to be attributable in part to shared family environment, socioeconomic status, education, and nutrition (see Mackintosh, 2011; Nisbett et al., 2012; Schaie, 1994, 2005; Staff et al., 2012). The role of environmental support in developing intelligence has important implications for education and parenting, providing one empirical basis for many early intervention programs. This environmental evidence gives us reason for optimism. Picking good parents isn't everything.

Ultimately, though, it would be very difficult, if not impossible, for us to tell you if nature or nurture is more important to intelligence. The complexities of that discussion go far, far beyond the scope of this book. We think it will be better for you to come away with the understanding that conceptualizing the argument as "nature versus nurture" sets the debate off on the wrong path. It is much better to think of it instead as "nature *via* nurture" (see Ridley, 2003; see also Blair & Raver, 2012; Bronfenbrenner & Ceci, 1994). Both nature and nurture contribute to the development of intelligence, and nature and nurture impact each other in a recursive way. You can't really distinguish the importance of the length versus the width of a rectangle when calculating its area, right?

And so it is with the FE. Perhaps inquiries into its causes and consequences will help us to discover if the observed gains in IQ score represent actual gains in human intelligence, shed light on the causes of those gains, and help society navigate the implications of a rising IQ. These implications have already proven to have profound consequences for students receiving special education services and for capital offenders. If it turns out that the persistent, worldwide gains in IQ represent real gains in human intelligence, there are even greater implications for the future of our species itself.

TAKEAWAYS

- Flynn's causal explanation of the FE as a nurture effect—a change in society's orientation toward abstract thinking as a result of exposure to scientific technology—may not be supported by the data to the degree he suggests.
- Many scholars offer alternative explanations for the FE, including improvements in nutrition, advances in public health, better education, the environment in general, or genetics.
- Some researchers argue that the FE is a statistical or methodological artifact and does not represent any real gains in intelligence.
- Heritability estimates for intellectual abilities generally fall between 40% and 60%.
- It is better to think of nature *via* nurture rather than nature *versus* nurture.

NOTES

1. Observers have noted that Flynn may not have been the first person to observe this phenomenon (e.g., Thorndike, 1977), but Flynn appears to have been the first scholar to systematically look across multiple data sets in multiple countries to note the pattern of rising scores across standardization samples.
2. Alan S. Kaufman's contribution to the Psychology 101 series, *IQ Testing 101* (2009), describes the norming processes in considerable detail. Readers who are interested in learning more about norming procedures should consult his book.
3. *Mentally retarded* is the term used in *Atkins v. Virginia*, rather than the newer designation *person with an intellectual or developmental disability*.
4. And neither did Watson. When people share this quote, they usually leave off the next sentence: "I am going beyond my facts and I admit it, but so have the advocates of the contrary and they have been doing it for many thousands of years" (p. 82).

A Brief Interlude on Race

This is not a section we wanted to write. Why, then, you ask, would you write it and make us read it? Well, the editors made us add it![1] But actually, we had our reasons for not dwelling on race and intelligence. First and foremost, so much of intelligence theory's more controversial aspects have been tied to race, making the broader concept of intelligence a toxic subject to many people. Our initial thinking was that we should avoid a strong focus on racial issues in intelligence so as not to further reinforce the often ugly historical relationship between race and intelligence. So much of the general topic of intelligence is fascinating and provocative without dealing with its most controversial aspects, why divert your attention from the cool stuff?[2]

Another, more selfish reason is that racism is a tough topic for academics to tackle. The potential to misspeak or write statements that are too imprecise—and therefore open to misinterpretation—is very high, in part because almost all discussions of race are emotionally charged. In our experience, when things get emotional, they get personal; and when they get personal, the dispassionate analysis we prefer usually goes out the window.

When our editors suggested that we reconsider our decision to address race only indirectly in this book, the first author (Jonathan) recalled a conversation he had a year earlier with the eminent scholar Donna Ford, a professor at Vanderbilt who has long called attention to the racism faced by many students in our education system and society. After speaking on a panel with Jonathan at a briefing for policymakers, she pulled him aside and said, "You need to keep talking about race; people need to hear your voice on these issues." To which he replied, "But Donna, it's so uncomfortable for me as a White male. I'm worried my words will be twisted, or that people will say I don't understand the situation, since I'm a White dude. And I am a very White dude." Donna, who has a great sense of humor, paused, narrowed her eyes, and said, "Yes, all those things will probably happen. But that doesn't mean you don't try." After a dramatic pause, she eyed him up and down and then said, "And you are very, very White." Touché, Professor Ford, touché.

So let's talk about race.

Putting the emotional aspects of the topic aside for a moment, the issue's complexity for academics is partly self-inflicted; they often twist themselves into knots when they make tortured arguments related to race and culture. The eminent geographer Jared Diamond is a case in point. In his Pulitzer Prize–winning *Guns, Germs and Steel*, an examination of why human societies differ, he notes:

> Probably the commonest explanation involves . . . assuming biological differences among peoples. . . . Today, segments of Western society publicly repudiate racism. Yet many (perhaps most!)

> Westerners continue to accept [these] racist explanations privately or subconsciously. . . . The objection to such racist explanations is not just that they are loathsome, but also that they are wrong. (Diamond, 1999, pp. 18–19)

Okay, definitely not a "nature" guy! Calling the other side racists is coarse but understandable from his theoretical perspective, and it's hard to argue with his basic observation. Yet he then eviscerates his argument by noting, "In fact, . . . modern 'Stone Age' peoples are on average probably more intelligent, not less intelligent, than industrialized peoples" (p. 19). He goes on to repeat this assertion a few more times. Granted, at the end of the book he notes unequivocally that he believes long-term differences in societal development are due to environmental factors and not innate differences. But by even suggesting that intelligence strongly differs across societies, he fuels the debate he's trying to end, in a way. Two steps forward, one step back.

In earlier chapters, we discussed the ugly eugenic application of intelligence theory and research in the late 19th and early 20th centuries, a legacy we are still dealing with today. And although we like to pretend that this particular bit of nastiness quickly disappeared,[3] controversies about intelligence, race, and gender flare up about once every generation or two, with the publication of *The Bell Curve* in 1994 and the Richwine affair in 2013 being cases in point.[4] Over the decades, researchers and theorists have implied or directly stated that non-White people, women, poor people, uneducated people, people with disabilities, the Irish, and many other demographic groups are less intelligent than other groups, often proposing rather severe remedies for the situation (many of which assumed that the alleged low intelligence was hereditary in nature). As we've emphasized throughout this book, students of intelligence should keep the historical context in mind. But that is a two-way street, as we also have to keep the historical context in mind when people bristle at the word *intelligence*. When some parents express reluctance to have their children tested, psychologists and teachers should be sensitive to their concerns. They've heard the stories too, often from their grandparents and parents, if not having directly experienced racism, sexism, classism, and other forms of bias with education and other human services, broadly defined.

There are two primary questions to be answered here:

1. Do measures of intelligence reveal differences between demographic groups in intelligence test scores?
2. If so, are those differences genetic or environmental in nature?

The answer to the first question is usually yes. Even many "culture-free" or "culture-fair" tests find evidence of demographic differences. But the second question has been hotly debated for over a century, and we don't see that changing any time soon. That said, Hunt's (2012) summary of the situation strikes us as being fair, based on the available evidence:

> Some psychologists have taken very strong views about the hypothesis that differences in [general cognitive ability] between racial-ethnic groups have a genetic origin. . . . Two of the most vocal proponents of the genetic hypothesis have this to say: "Genetic and cultural factors carry the exact same weight in causing the mean Black-White difference in IQ as they do in causing individual differences in IQ, about 80% genetic–20% environmental by adulthood" (Rushton & Jensen, 2005, p. 279). An opponent of the genetic hypothesis has examined the evidence and concluded that "For the race differences in IQ, we can be confident that genes play no role at all (Nisbett, 2009, p. 197). Neither of these extreme statements can be justified. (p. 302)

So race differences in intelligence test scores—and while we're at it, let's throw gender and socioeconomic status into the mix— exist, but we do not know why. Are the differences due to genetics? Are environmental factors influencing intellectual development? Is there cultural bias in the test items and testing context? We suspect that most researchers, if pressed, would profess to a hybrid position: part genetic, part environmental, part test bias, with the interaction between the first two sets of factors being most important. Are those genetic influences based on race or gender or social class? Maybe, maybe not. However, let us suggest an alternative proposition: The causes of these differences do not matter very much, at least from an educational or policy perspective.

Hernnstein and Murray (1994) would have a conniption fit if they heard us say that, and so would Rushton and Jensen (2005), who boldly stated, "Denial of any genetic component in human variation, including between groups, is not only poor science, it is likely to be injurious both to unique individuals and to the complex structure of societies" (p. 285). Rushton and Jensen were never ones to pull punches, but hold on a second. Certainly very few people dispute that there is "any genetic component in human variation," but to say that people who won't generalize that to racial groups are poor scientists is a pretty big logical leap.

For argument's sake, we won't dispute that differences in tested intelligence exist between groups defined by race, gender, ethnicity, and other demographics.[5] Rushton and Jensen estimate the White–Black IQ difference to be 15 points, roughly one standard deviation.[6] That, quite frankly, is a big difference. So big, in fact, that it calls to mind the results of Goddard's tests of Ellis Island immigrants mentioned in an earlier chapter. Recall that Goddard found such poor results for certain immigrant groups that even he started to question the genetic basis of ethnic group differences. When group differences are large enough to be shocking, red flags should pop up in scientists' minds.

As a case in point, consider recent research on excellence gaps. Plucker, Burroughs, and Song (2010) examined national and state achievement test scores to determine if racial differences existed in the percentages of students who scored at the highest achievement levels.[7] They found stark differences between

White, Black, and Hispanic students. For example, on the grade 4 mathematics test in 2011, 9% of White students scored at the advanced level, compared with 2% of Hispanic and 1% of Black students. Perhaps more important, the percentages in 1996 were 3% White, 0.1% Black, and 0.2% Hispanic: The gaps widened considerably over less than a generation. Given these huge differences in educational outcomes, do you care if there's a genetic component to these differences? Probably not, and furthermore, you would probably note that it is essentially impossible that White elementary school students could suddenly start to gain supposed genetic superiority between 2000 and 2003, when the percentage of advanced scores started to rise. Therefore, environmental factors are probably the cause of most observed excellence gaps, and nurture-based solutions are just as clearly the main strategy for tackling these gaps.

In closing, as Hunt (2012) points out, differences between groups may have very different causes: Paraphrasing Hunt's example, our friends in Rotterdam (the Netherlands) and Accra (Ghana) differ in many ways, with physical appearance having a strong genetic flavor. But language differences probably have a strong environmental component. To complicate things further, consider whether eons of human evolution could be influenced by the environment, leading to genetic differences over time. Untangling the reasons behind these differences is an interesting, complex scientific pursuit, but at the end of the day, our Dutch and Ghanaian friends look different from each other and talk to each other in English. We're back to finding the area of the rectangle.

Claiming the existence of genetic differences in intelligence due to race is the scientific equivalent of throwing a Molotov cocktail into public discourse. Doing so may bring notoriety, but it is horribly insensitive to the often nasty history of race and intelligence, and it feeds the flames in people who use such comments to justify discrimination or worse policies and behaviors (the Richwine controversy in 2013 revolved around the issue of immigration reform). And in the end, whether genetic differences in intelligence truly exist due to race (or gender, or socioeconomic status, etc.) probably has no practical implication for your daily life.

TAKEAWAYS

- Differences in measured intelligence exist between groups based on gender, race, and other demographic characteristics.
- These differences tend to emerge even on "culture fair" tests of intelligence.
- What the differences mean is hotly debated, with no consensus among researchers.
- General differences in intelligence likely have a genetic component, but extending the genetic argument to race and ethnicity is tricky.
- In the end, for the vast majority of people, knowing the "true cause" of demographic differences in intelligence probably doesn't matter very much.

NOTES

1. Seriously, they did. But they were right, we couldn't duck the topic.
2. Another, more practical reason is that Alan Kaufman, in *IQ Testing 101*, covers the topic comprehensively and effectively.
3. The well-known comedian Louis C.K. was on a late-night talk show when he observed that some Americans like to pretend that slavery happened hundreds of years ago; yet it's only

140 years in the past or, as he noted, "two 70-year-olds ago." We need to keep in mind that systematic, de jure racism was the law of the land for many years, as recently as the 1960s. There are millions of Americans alive today who literally lived with the law telling them they could be "separate but equal."

4. Jason Richwine, co-author of an anti-immigration report published by the Heritage Foundation, was recently revealed to have written a dissertation for his Harvard PhD that argued for White–Hispanic differences in intelligence. Predictably, a firestorm ensued, and even the Heritage Foundation distanced itself from him.

5. Although we are not saying this *can't* be disputed, depending on which definitions and assessments are being used. See, for example, D'Amico, Cardaci, Di Nuovo, and Naglieri, 2012; Naglieri, Rojahn, and Matto, 2007.

6. A fierce debate rages about whether nonverbal intelligence tests find smaller (or nonexistent) group differences, especially within the context of identifying intellectual giftedness. Some scholars say they do (e.g., Naglieri & Ford, 2003, 2005), and others think that argument is overstated (e.g., Lohman, 2005). However, a nuanced third position has emerged, positing that certain *types* of nonverbal questions may be race neutral, and that future nonverbal assessments should not treat each type of nonverbal item similarly (Lohman & Gambrell, 2012).

7. For example, on the primary national test, the U.S. Department of Education's National Assessment of Educational Progress, the levels are Below Basic, Basic, Proficient, and Advanced.

Creativity and Giftedness

e know what you're thinking: Why include a chapter on creativity and giftedness in an introductory book on human intelligence? This material is important for a few reasons. First, many treatments of psychological topics do not address so-called positive psychology, that is, psychological strengths. Second, and no less important, we suspect that when most people think of an "intelligent person," they are often thinking in terms of intellectual and creative giftedness. As we mentioned early on in this book, definitions of constructs are important things, and clearly differentiating between intelligence and related constructs such as creativity and intellectual giftedness helps us to better understand each construct.

In a related vein, people find the relationships among these constructs to be interesting, and they continue to attract

111

the attention of both researchers and the general public. These constructs are also highly interrelated in practice, with most major theories of giftedness, for example, involving intelligence and creativity. As Sternberg and O'Hara (1999) note, the intelligence–creativity relationship is "theoretically important, and its answer probably affects the lives of countless children and adults" (p. 269). For these reasons, the (potential) overlap among these constructs raises lots of practical questions about education, management, and human resources: Is a highly intelligent person more or less likely to be creative? What is the relationship between high levels of intelligence and social skills, especially the ability to solve problems via social interaction? How does intelligence translate to real-world success in the classroom, on the athletic field, in the boardroom, and in the broader community?

INTELLIGENCE AND CREATIVITY

In general, theory and research on this topic are murky and often downright contradictory. For example, the threshold theory suggests intelligence is a necessary but not a sufficient condition for creativity (Barron, 1969; Yamamoto, 1964a, 1964b), certification theory focuses on environmental factors that allow people to display creativity and intelligence (Hayes, 1989), and an interference hypothesis suggests that very high levels of intelligence may interfere with creativity (Simonton, 1994; Sternberg, 1996). The researchers cited above all do (or did) very high-quality work, so one can be forgiven for reading these different perspectives and asking, "Huh?"

To help clarify the situation, Sternberg (1999a) proposed a way to classify the various approaches to studying the intelligence–creativity relationship. We have always liked this framework, primarily because it acknowledges the importance of construct definitions that we discuss throughout this book. Sternberg's model suggests five possible relationships: creativity as a subset of intelligence, intelligence as a subset of creativity, creativity and intelligence as overlapping sets, creativity and intelligence as coincident sets, and creativity and intelligence as disjoint sets. In the following sections, we provide examples of the first three types of relationships (the last two categories, coincident and disjoint sets, are not common and are not described here).

Creativity as a Subset of Intelligence

A number of psychometric theories include creativity, either explicitly or implicitly, as a part of intelligence. Guilford's Structure of the Intellect (SOI) model is probably the most explicit, with divergent thinking specifically identified as one of his five cognitive operations. This model was influential in educational circles (Meeker, 1969), and Renzulli (1973) developed an entire creativity curriculum based on the aspects of the SOI model involving divergent thinking. As early as 1912 Henmon directly connected intelligence and creativity, observing that

> [t]he scholarly or erudite man who has merely acquired knowledge created by others may not represent as high a degree of intelligence as one who is independent, original and productive in his thinking, but we should scarcely say that he is unintelligent. Intelligence is indicated by the capacity to appropriate truth and fact as well as by the capacity to discover them. (1912/1969, p. 16)

Gardner (1993), coming at the constructs from his developmental and qualitative angle, has used multiple intelligences (MI) theory to study creativity, among other constructs such as leadership, implicitly suggesting that creativity is a subset of MI theory. Cattell–Horn–Carroll (CHC) theory—which, as noted in Chapter 5, is a combination of the Cattell–Horn theory of fluid and crystallized intelligence (Horn & Cattell, 1966a, 1967; Horn & Noll, 1997) and Carroll's (1993) three-stratum theory—includes creativity and originality as components of long-term storage and retrieval of information (*Glr*).

Intelligence as a Subset of Creativity

In contrast, other researchers have hypothesized that intelligence is a part of creativity. Though it is not a dominant view among intelligence theories (not surprisingly!), recent examples of this approach include Sternberg and Lubart's (1995) investment theory of creativity, which emphasizes the role of intelligence and knowledge, and Amabile's (1996) componential theory of creativity, which includes domain-specific and domain-general intellectual abilities.

Overlapping Sets

Sternberg's third grouping conceptualizes intelligence and creativity as overlapping yet distinct constructs. Renzulli's (1978) Three-Ring Conception of giftedness theorizes that giftedness—implicitly cast as high-level creative production—is caused by the overlap of high intellectual ability, creativity, and task commitment. From this perspective, creativity and intelligence are distinct constructs but overlap considerably under the right conditions. In a similar vein, the concept of planning abilities in PASS theory appears to overlap with creativity (Naglieri & Kaufman, 2001); and Plucker, Beghetto, and Dow (2004) view creativity and intelligence as related but distinct in their definition of creativity as "the interaction among aptitude, process, and environment by which an individual or group produces a perceptible product that is both novel and useful as defined within a social context" (p. 90).

Threshold Theory. Traditional research has argued for a threshold theory, in which creativity and intelligence are positively, if moderately, correlated up to an IQ of approximately 120; in people with higher IQs, the two constructs show little relationship (e.g., Fuchs-Beauchamp, Karnes, & Johnson, 1993; Getzels & Jackson, 1962). Sternberg places this perspective in the "overlapping sets" category. This view is so common as to be considered part of the conventional wisdom about creativity, intelligence, and giftedness.

There is one small problem with this widely held belief: It's probably wrong. Several empirical studies call into question the presence of any threshold, whether lower or higher than a 120 IQ (Kim, 2005; Preckel, Holling, & Weise, 2006). However, many of these studies use group intelligence tests or have become quite dated. For example, Kim (2005), who reanalyzed data from several previous studies, used data from some studies that were over 30 years old—from intelligence tests that, by definition, do not reflect current theory. Other studies have defined creativity rather narrowly as divergent thinking, or the ability to generate multiple ideas in response to a single prompt.[1]

Fortunately, researchers have begun to address these limitations, with interesting results. For example, Sligh, Conners, and Roskos-Ewoldsen (2005) used a contemporary measure of intelligence, the Kaufman Adolescent and Adult Intelligence Scale (Kaufman & Kaufman, 1993), and a measure of creative innovation to examine the relationship between intelligence and creativity. By assessing both Gc and Gf, they were able to show moderate, positive correlations between Gc and creativity (i.e., similar to previous studies); however, intelligence and creativity were significantly correlated for the high-IQ group, but they were not significantly correlated for people with average intelligence scores—the opposite of the pattern that threshold theory predicts.

A similar set of studies, with a much different population, reached similar conclusions. The Study of Mathematically Precocious Youth has been following a cohort of students from late childhood/early adolescence into adulthood. These students all scored in the top 1% on college entrance examinations before the age of 13, so they are a very bright group. Park, Lubinski, and Benbow (2007, 2008) found that, within this very intelligent group, intellectual talent was highly correlated with educational attainment. This by itself is not surprising, but they also found that a range of indicators of adult creative accomplishments (e.g., patents, publications, awards) were also correlated with intelligence. These results, emerging as they do from studies that address the limitations of previous research, raise serious doubts about the threshold effect.

Recent research by Beaty and Silvia (2012) provides some insight into the mechanisms in play here. They had college students complete a standard divergent thinking test over a 10-minute period, and they found—as in much previous research—that the students reported more creative ideas as time marched on. However, they also administered a measure of fluid intelligence, and—surprisingly—the higher the Gf score, the flatter the slope of the creativity–time curve. In other words, the most intelligent people in their sample did not come up with appreciably more creative ideas over time, but rather provided fairly creative ideas from the beginning to the end of the 10 minutes. Less intelligent participants had increasingly steep slopes, meaning that they definitely were more creative as time progressed. This study provides intriguing evidence that there is an underlying cognitive basis behind recent observations that intelligence and creativity are correlated even at high levels of intelligence, and that those underlying mechanisms may be a combination of executive processes related to information retrieval and manipulation and associative processes that involve activation of various parts of one's cognitive schema (i.e., how you organize knowledge in your brain).

INTELLIGENCE AND GIFTEDNESS

The relationship between intelligence and giftedness has also received substantial attention. Nearly every gifted education program has a formal assessment procedure to identify potential participants, and creativity assessments are often included in the battery of measures in these identification systems.

For example, in a comprehensive study of school districts' giftedness identification systems, Callahan, Hunsaker, Adams, Moore, and Bland (1995) found that "[t]he area of general intellectual ability was the most widely adopted construct. . . . Group tests of intelligence are still the most widely used assessment tools to assess this construct with individual tests . . . used as supplemental instruments" (p. 70).

As we have noted repeatedly, definitions of constructs matter a great deal, and the ambiguity that accompanies the construct of giftedness is similar to that associated with intelligence and creativity. For example, are giftedness and talent the same thing, or are they independent? If independent, do they overlap at all? Given that nearly all states have laws on gifted education, one would expect that the relevant legislation would at least contain some consistency regarding definitions of what makes someone "gifted." However, in the last comprehensive analysis of this topic, Passow and Rudnitski (1993) found that state statutes and policies were inconsistent in their definitions and levels of detail.

Case law on gifted education is similarly muddy, due in part to a lack of understanding on the part of the legal community about what giftedness and gifted education actually represent (Decker, Eckes, & Plucker, 2010; Eckes & Plucker, 2005; Plucker, 2008). The last federal report on this topic contained a somewhat ambiguous definition (OERI, 1993), which did not resolve the issue, and the lack of a standard definition and the breadth of talents available have led to the existence of many theories and definitions of giftedness (see Passow, 1979; Robinson, Zigler, & Gallagher, 2000; Sternberg & Davidson, 1986), although two frameworks have been suggested for organizing these conceptions: Sternberg and Davidson (1986) proposed four categories (explicit: domain-specific, explicit: cognitive, explicit: developmental, implicit: theoretical), and Mönks and Mason (1993) proposed four different groupings (trait-oriented, cognitive component, achievement-oriented, sociocultural/psychosocial-oriented). However, we believe that a simpler, two-category approach (early conceptions versus contemporary approaches) is sufficient to provide a sense of how the concept of giftedness has developed.

Early Conceptions

The Unitary Model. As the construct of giftedness—and its educational applications via gifted education—developed over the course of the 21st century, many of the earliest conceptions emerged from theories that viewed intelligence as a personal construct residing within the individual. Although many of these theories, ranging from monocentric and related approaches (Cattell, 1987; Spearman, 1904) to differentiated models (Carroll, 1993; Guilford, 1967; Thurstone, 1938), acknowledge the role of the environment in the development of intelligence, the focus is firmly placed on the individual as the locus of control and unit of interest. Theories and models of creativity from this time similarly accented the individual (e.g., Guilford, 1950; Kris, 1952; MacKinnon, 1965), and the vast majority of this work was heavily influenced by psychometrics.

The early conceptions of giftedness mirrored this emphasis on the individual and psychometrics (e.g., Hollingworth, 1942), and approaches to talent development based on these traditional conceptions of intelligence remain popular. For example, the

Talent Search model initiated at Johns Hopkins University now works with more than 250,000 children per year (at varying levels of service) at several university-based regional centers across the country (Stanley, 1980; Stanley & Benbow, 1981). Many school districts nationwide base their gifted education and talent development programs on the identification of high-ability children using instruments focused primarily on each individual's capabilities; in their national study, Callahan et al. (1995) found that 11% of the surveyed districts relied on a strict IQ definition of giftedness, making it the second most common definition. Robinson (2005) provides a detailed defense of psychometric approaches, although her analysis suggests that strict "you're as gifted as your total IQ score" identification systems are not the only approach to psychometrically based, unitary approaches to gifted education.

The Marland Definition. The federal government proposed a definition in the early 1970s that appears to have been based on the person-specific view of giftedness. This definition suggests that giftedness and talent are manifest in six areas: general intellectual ability, specific academic aptitude, creative or productive thinking, leadership ability, visual and performing arts, and psychomotor ability (Marland, 1972). The Marland definition has been extremely influential and is still used by many school districts in their identification of talented students. Callahan et al. (1995) found that nearly 50% of districts based their gifted education identification procedures on this definition, making it far and away the most popular definition in this setting.

Contemporary Approaches

Contemporary approaches are primarily characterized by broadened conceptions of intellectual giftedness. Beginning in the mid- to late 1970s, scholars proposed a number of new conceptions of giftedness that were more developmental, contextual, and multifaceted than earlier models. This trend ran parallel to the broadening of theories of intelligence reviewed in Chapter 5. For example, perhaps the best-known theory of giftedness, Renzulli's (1978, 1999) Three-Ring Conception, focuses on the interaction among above-average ability, creativity, and task commitment, within the context of personality, environmental, and affective factors.

Educational approaches to talent development based on these broader theories include Renzulli and Reis's (1985) School-wide Enrichment Model and several of the strategies described in Coleman and Cross (2001), Karnes and Bean (2001), and Plucker and Callahan (2008, 2013). Other contemporary definitions of giftedness and talent (Feldhusen, 1998; OERI, 1993) are similar in spirit to Renzulli's Three-Ring Conception and related pro-gramming models with an emphasis on broadened conceptions and acknowledgment of multiple influences on the development of talent.

In most of these broader conceptions, intelligence is men-tioned or implied in some form. However, in contrast to ear-lier conceptions that saw giftedness and intelligence as largely synonymous, contemporary views tend to see high levels of intelligence as a necessary but not sufficient condition for gifted-ness. In the remainder of this chapter, we describe five distinct conceptions of giftedness to provide some examples of how major thinkers view the intelligence–giftedness relationship.

The Differentiated Model of Giftedness and Talent. One of the more pragmatic models of giftedness is the Differentiated Model of Giftedness and Talent (DMGT; Gagné, 1993, 2000). The DMGT conceptualizes gifts as innate abilities in at least one domain area (i.e., intellectual, creative, socioaffective, or sensorimotor) that place the individual in the top 10% of age peers (Gagné, 2000). Talent, on the other hand, is the demonstrated mastery of the gift as evidenced by skills in academics, arts, business, leisure, social action, sports, or technology that place the individual in the top 10% of age peers. Gifts are the potential; talents are the outcomes.

According to the DMGT, a person can have a natural ability to excel—that is, be identified as gifted—without manifesting actual talent (i.e., underachievement). Talent development involves the systematic learning and practice needed for skills to be maximized, with higher-order skills requiring more intense and longer-term development (Gagné, 2000).

Gifts alone do not account for all the variance in talent development, which is a process mediated by intrapersonal and environmental catalysts, which can either support or hinder the development of talent (Gagné, 2000). The DMGT focuses on variables that can both hurt and help the fostering of talent, more realistically modeling real-world talent development compared with earlier models that focus on positive talent development. Intrapersonal catalysts include both physical (handicaps, health, etc.) and psychological characteristics (motivation, volition, self-management, and personality). Environmental catalysts include physical, cultural, familial, and social influences; people such as parents, teachers, peers, and mentors; provisions (programs, activities, services); and events (encounters, awards, accidents, etc.). It is also important to note that chance does play a role in genetic endowment as well as in talent development—for example, the good fortune of being born into a family and community that are willing and able to support the development of skills (Gagné, 2000).

Intellectual ability is specifically mentioned as one of four aptitude domains, along with creativity, socioaffective, and sensorimotor. Gagné refers to these four areas as natural abilities but does not provide a detailed model of intellectual aptitude. To his credit, he notes that "many competing classification systems exist" for each of four domains of natural talent, and he does not appear to prefer one over the others for the purposes of his model (2005, p. 101).

The Three-Ring Conception. The focus of Renzulli's work has been the creation of educational systems that help young people develop the skills, habits, and affect necessary for real-world creative productivity. Renzulli's (1978, 2005) Three-Ring Conception views giftedness as emerging from the interaction of well-above-average ability, creativity, and task commitment, with each characteristic playing a critical role in the development of gifted behavior. Renzulli and his colleagues have conducted a number of studies on the validity of the Three-Ring Conception (e.g., Delisle & Renzulli, 1982; Gubbins, 1982; Renzulli, 1984, 1988), including studies of the effectiveness of educational interventions on which the model is based. The theory remains among the most popular conceptions of giftedness in the literature and in school districts (Callahan et al., 1995).

This theory is based upon studies of talented, successful adults (Renzulli, 1978, 1999) and—although not without its critics (e.g., Johnsen, 1999; Kitano, 1999; Olszewski-Kubilius, 1999)—benefits from its inclusion of multiple interacting factors and the broadening of the criteria used in selection of gifted students. In addition, Renzulli emphasizes the need to develop creative productive skills in addition to knowledge acquisition, and presents evidence that his broadened identification procedures do indeed reduce inequalities such as a disproportionate representation of minorities in gifted education programs and gender equity (Renzulli, 1999).[2] Perhaps the major contribution of the Three-Ring Conception—and the many related educational interventions that emerged from this model—is that it helped destroy the widely held belief that creativity was innate and could not be increased. The model also reinforced the role of intellectual ability, in combination with task commitment, in the processes leading to creative productivity.

MI Theory. As noted in Chapter 5, Gardner's theory of multiple intelligences was a major milestone in encouraging educators to adopt broader definitions of human intelligence, and of human capabilities more generally. His definition of intelligence as "an ability or set of abilities that permit an individual to solve problems or fashion products that are of consequence in a particular cultural setting" (Ramos-Ford & Gardner, 1997, p. 55) has obvious appeal to educators working with talented students, and MI theory's popularity within gifted education (especially in the 1990s) is not surprising.

Moreover, MI theory represents an important shift in expanding what might be considered intelligent behavior and thus has the possibility of broadening the representations of giftedness. Although much of Gardner's work with the theory has been focused on creative production and giftedness (see Gardner, 1993), MI theory's broadening of the construct of intelligence was very appealing to educators of gifted students who wished to expand the ways in which students are considered to be gifted and talented.

> Although MI theory's popularity peaked after the research by Callahan et al. (1995) was conducted in the early 1990s, anecdotal evidence suggests that the theory was enormously influential in changing educators' conceptions of intelligence, creativity, and talent. However, assessment within applied education settings has proven to be complex and fraught with difficulties, potentially limiting its impact on the identification of creativity within gifted identification systems (see, e.g., Gardner, 1995; Plucker, 2000; Plucker, Callahan, & Tomchin, 1996; Pyryt, 2000). That said, similar to Renzulli's larger impact on education, Gardner's work has indisputably helped broaden our conceptions of what talent and giftedness are and where they can be found.

The Situated View. Around the turn of the century, a variety of newer philosophical perspectives were heavily influencing views of learning and talent. Many psychologists and educators were growing weary of conceptualizations that described constructs, including intelligence, talent, and creativity, as being either largely cognitive or environmental. In response to this dissatisfaction, Barab and Plucker (2002) reviewed theory and research within five such perspectives (ecological psychology, situated cognition, distributed cognition, activity theory, and legitimate peripheral participation) and concluded that "the separation of mind and context at the heart of traditional conceptions of talent development polarizes learner and context, either implicitly or explicitly stating that, in the case of talent and giftedness, the individual impacts or influences the environment" (Plucker & Barab, 2005, p. 204). In a similar vein, Snow (1992) criticized the "tendency to think of persons and situations as independent variables, rather than persons-in-situations as integrated systems" (p. 19).

Barab and Plucker proposed an integrated model of giftedness in which talents, broadly defined, are developed through the interactions of the individual, environment, and sociocultural content. They viewed talent development as an ever-spiraling process, with continuing interactions building on themselves over time, leading to greater opportunities to develop talent—and greater success as a result of those efforts. The primary educational implication is that solving real-world problems, within realistic contexts and with considerable support, should be the focus of talent development programs (Plucker & Barab, 2005). That this situated view has proven to be more popular outside of the field of the gifted education than within makes sense, given that many gifted education programs primarily use an "identify the bright kid" intervention model, which Barab and Plucker's approach explicitly argues against.

Subotnik and Colleagues' Approach. The latest major development is the conceptual model proposed by Subotnik, Olszewski-Kubilius, and Worrell (2011, 2012; Worrell, Olszewski- Kubilius, & Subotnik, 2012). After an exhaustive summary of psychological research on giftedness, they define giftedness as "performance that is clearly at the upper end of the distribution in a specific talent domain even relative to other high-functioning individuals in that domain. Further, giftedness can be viewed as developmental in that in the beginning stages, potential is the key variable; in later stages, achievement is the measure of giftedness; and in fully developed talents, eminence is the basis on which this label is granted" (Subotnik et al., 2012, p. 176).

This approach is appealing for a number of reasons. First and foremost, it explicitly states how the definition of the construct changes as people develop (i.e., a construct can be context-dependent and still be quite workable). Subotnik et al. also emphasize that giftedness results from a combination of cognitive and psychosocial variables, in keeping with the theme of broad-based influences on giftedness that we see across all contemporary conceptions. They also endorse Dweck's view, described in Chapter 5, that intelligence is malleable and that beliefs about intelligence matter. The practical implications of their model run parallel to their definition:

> Although we recognize that the generation of creative performances or ideas requires person, process, and product, it is also the case that the relative emphasis on these factors shifts over time. For example, it is important that young children develop a creative approach and attitude (person), that older children acquire skills (process), and that the acquisition of these mindsets and process skills are then coupled with deep multidisciplinary content knowledge and are applied to the creation of intellectual, aesthetic, or practical products or performances (product). (Subotnik et al., 2011, p. 33)

This approach to interventions reinforces the situated view of Barab and Plucker but extends it by noting that the relative contributions of the parts of the person–environment–sociocultural interaction may vary over time and across different contexts.

SUMMARY

Like theories of intelligence, the related but distinct constructs of creativity and giftedness have developed over time. Their relationship with intelligence is conceptualized in many ways, but we need to remember that creativity and giftedness are also psychological constructs, and a wide range of definitions have been offered for each construct. Their definitions matter not only for understanding creativity and giftedness, but also for understanding how those concepts relate to intelligence.

When considering practical applications, such as identifying students for participation in specific programs, how one defines each construct should be the first consideration when deciding how to identify or select students for the program. For example, using a nonverbal intelligence test to help identify students for a program for high-ability writers may not be appropriate, but using such a test for a program that seeks to develop a wider range of talents may make perfect sense. Once again, context and definitions matter.

TAKEAWAYS

- There are different ways to view the relationship between intelligence and creativity. How one defines each construct has a big impact on how one views the intelligence–creativity relationship.
- Each of Sternberg's five hypothesized relationships has some empirical support, which is not surprising given the construct definition issues.
- The threshold theory proposes that intelligence and creativity are correlated up to a certain level of intelligence, above which the correlation becomes minimal.

- Some recent studies suggest that the threshold theory is incorrect, and that intelligence and creativity may be correlated even at very high levels of intelligence.
- Just as theories of intelligence have become multifaceted and multidimensional over the past 40 to 50 years, so have theories of giftedness and talent.
- Educators designing systems for identifying high levels of creativity and intelligence among students should consider how their chosen conception of giftedness defines these terms and their relationship. In other words, a program identifying giftedness based on Renzulli's model, MI theory, or Barab and Plucker's situated perspective shouldn't be using an individually administered intelligence test as its sole indicator of talent, intelligence, and creativity.

NOTES

1. See, for example, Jauk, Benedek, Dunst, and Neubauer (2013).
2. Renzulli has significantly—and importantly—broadened his model, but a full description is beyond the scope of our current discussion. See Renzulli and Sytsma (2008) and Renzulli and D'Souza (2013) for more information.

Constructs ᴀɴᴅ Contexts: Where Is the Studᴜ of Intelligence Heading?

ver the past 20 years we have greatly enjoyed being unofficial historians of the psychology of intelligence. Interacting with the wide range of personalities and perspectives in the field alone has been worth the hard work,[1] and we've learned a great deal about theoretical approaches to intelligence and how a scientific field develops.

For example, *The Mismeasure of Man* (Gould, 1981) and *The Bell Curve* (Herrnstein & Murray, 1994) both remain highly controversial books, representing as they do two ends of a continuum about the nature of the origins of intelligence and, as a result, eliciting strident criticism (e.g., Carroll, 1995; Devlin, Fienberg, Resnick, & Roeder, 1997). But it can be argued that each book pushed debates about intelligence, talent, and human ability to the forefront of public conversation, reinforcing the principle that one valuable role of academics and other researchers is to push the envelopes of debate over important topics.

In a similar vein, we also learned a great deal about how many of the researchers and theorists view each other's work. For example, when one eminent scholar viewed our initial material for the human intelligence website (www.intelltheory.com), he openly questioned our assertion that one scholar influenced another, noting, "The two of them never agreed on anything." Yet when we returned to the research, we noted that the younger scholar cited the older over a dozen times in his seminal work, primarily to contrast their approaches to the topic; no one said influence is purely positive! We have also had several experiences where researchers told us we have specific details wrong—when we had pulled the details in question straight from autobiographies or definitive biographies. These and similar instances reinforce for us the fact that history is, in the end, highly subjective, being perpetually rewritten and rethought by those who come after us. The historian exerts control over what is considered history, with "reality," "facts," and "opinions" being somewhat fungible.

That said, our goal in this book has been to share the rich history of intelligence theory and research, and to pass on some of the stories that have captivated us over the years. We simply couldn't include everything important on this topic, and you wouldn't have wanted to read it all. But we hope we provided an enticing look at the amazing questions that have been answered and those that have yet to be answered regarding human intelligence and ability. We've tried to step back and "reset" certain aspects of that history that have strayed too far from what probably happened, emphasizing the role of historical context. For example, Goddard is now viewed quite harshly, but it's worth noting that much of his work was done in an era when President Woodrow Wilson, now remembered as a progressive reformer, was aggressively implementing racial segregation policies throughout the federal government. Theorists and researchers do not operate in a vacuum, and their cultural and intellectual contexts influence their work as much as their work influences the culture.

FUTURE DIRECTIONS FOR INTELLIGENCE THEORY AND RESEARCH

With that in mind, we'd like to close the book with some thoughts about future directions for intelligence theory and research. Given our emphasis on historical context, we realize that any such predictions are something of a shot in the dark. In the words of Winston Churchill, "I always avoid prophesying beforehand because it is much better to prophesy after the event has already taken place" (1944, p. 7). But it seems safe to conclude that several emerging trends will continue and probably strengthen.

Intelligence and the Brain

First and foremost, the exponentially increasing development of technology will continue to influence both research and interventions involving intelligence. From a research perspective, neurological studies of intelligence that were in the realm of science fiction only a generation ago have become commonplace. We expect this focus on the brain to continue. An ambitious new project launched by President Barack Obama in April 2013 is the $100 million Brain Research Through Advancing Innovative Neurotechnologies (BRAIN) initiative, a grand venture supported by the National Institutes of Health, the U.S. Defense

Department, the National Science Foundation, and four private research institutes. This ambitious undertaking is aimed at providing a comprehensive map of the structure and function of the human brain (Alivisatos et al., 2012), and it is seen by many as being the intellectual successor to the Human Genome Project, which finished mapping the human genome in 2003 (NHGRI, 2003). It is thrilling to imagine what will come out of this, and it is reasonable to assume that some of what is discovered will have a direct impact on future directions for human intelligence research.

Exciting developments in neuroscience have already made it possible for 21st-century researchers to look within the brain to try to find the biological bases for human intelligence differences. Neuroscience-supported intelligence research up to this point has generally focused either on genetics or on brain imaging studies. So far no "intelligence gene" or set of genes has presented itself as being key to establishing the intellectual capacity of healthy individuals (and many folks have searched). However, approximately 300 genes have been identified as contributing to intellectually disabling conditions (Deary, Penke, & Johnson, 2010). Future findings from the new BRAIN initiative will complement extant understandings gleaned from the map of the human genome, and it is quite likely that future researchers will eventually identify a set of genes that are partially responsible for differences in human intelligence.

Brain imaging studies are also becoming more relevant to intelligence research. One area where this can help is in establishing definitively whether or not size matters. Do bigger brains make for smarter people? The cautious answer at this point is probably yes, although positive correlations involving head size or brain volume are generally pretty weak. Improvements in MRI technology, which uses superconducting magnets and radio waves to create 3-D images of the brain, will help future researchers look at the morphology of distinct brain regions and systems, and possibly come to firm conclusions about the relationship between the size or function of distinct brain regions and differences in intelligent human behavior. These findings could be the first step toward the development of medical interventions.

In Daniel Keyes's (1966) heartbreaking novel *Flowers for Algernon,* a man with an intellectual disability undergoes an experimental surgery that transforms him over time into a person with extraordinary intellectual gifts. The ethical and moral dilemmas presented in this story demonstrate a potential dark side to these extraordinary neuroscientific advances: If we find out that certain brain structures, genes, or conditions of neural functioning are directly related to human intellectual performance, there will be some individuals or institutions that advocate intervening with biological processes to engineer smarter people. (Galton would probably find this idea appealing, right?) Future generations will have to figure out whether this is a good idea, a bad idea, or—as we predict—both, depending on context and intentions. It is not hard for us to imagine that in the future there may be scandals akin to the 2012 Lance Armstrong Tour de France medal disqualification, where a *Jeopardy!* grand champion or a Rhodes scholar is stripped of honors because of evidence that she took intellectual performance–enhancing drugs. Then again, it is also not hard to imagine the joy and relief felt by a parent who learns that there are medical treatments that can improve the intellectual functioning of a child born with a severe disability.

These dilemmas are not really new. For decades schools and universities have been dealing with the issue of healthy students taking drugs for attention deficit disorder off-label in an attempt to improve their study habits and test performance (Hall, Irwin, Bowman, Frankenberger, & Jewett, 2005). And after all, having heard the preliminary reports that caffeine may boost intelligence by enhancing nerve connectivity in the brain, we are more than willing to chug a cup o' joe while writing this book (see Simons, Caruana, Zhao, & Dudek, 2011). (Pardon us while we each gulp our third cup this morning.) The day may come when the question of whether or not to take a "smart pill," undergo an invasive surgical procedure, or even choose the intellectual makeup of an embryo will be matters of personal ethical choice as well as public policy.

Technology and Education

Technology is also rapidly changing education. In addition to increased access to education via distance learning, the ability to collect, store, and analyze data about individual students' learning is improving. As society moves in the direction of individualized education, questions about how intelligence is conceptualized and assessed will move to the forefront of policy discussions.

Theory Development

We suspect that theories will continue to become more and more sensitive to context (e.g., the situated cognition approach), but the era of increasingly broad and inclusive theories may be nearing its end; one can only broaden a construct so much before reaching a point of diminishing returns. Gardner hints at this in his deliberations about expanding multiple intelligences theory to include additional components, such as religious intelligence.

In a recent analysis of empirical trends in intelligence research, Sternberg and Kaufman (2012) conclude that studies designed to expand conceptions of intelligence or improve our understanding of the nature of g will continue to appear (e.g., Kaufman et al., 2012), probably at the expense of more traditional studies aimed at identifying new correlates of g. That analysis feels accurate to us, given our caveat above about the natural limit to the usefulness of ever-expanding theories.

International Perspectives

We also foresee growth in international perspectives on intel-ligence, befitting the emphasis (and debates) over the past 3 decades on the importance of cultural context. It's worth noting that the major scholarly work on international perspectives on intelligence (Sternberg, Lautrey, & Lubart, 2003) includes authors only from the United States, Europe, and Australia. As we have seen in our own work, only a few years ago many of our Asian colleagues teaching about intelligence relied heavily on Western research and theory, and as the social sciences have advanced across Asian countries, more Asian perspectives are being taught and shared. Similarly, comparisons of intelligence and cognitive ability among nations will continue to fascinate both the public and scholars, in part because such comparison touches on an interesting set of issues (see Hunt, 2012) and in part due to the growth of globalization.

IT'S ALL ABOUT THE CONSTRUCTS

Throughout this book we have tried to emphasize the impor-tance of definitions in studying a psychological construct such as intelligence. Definitions really do matter. At the risk of beating this theme to death, we want to share one more example.

When the book *The Bell Curve* was published in 1994, it cre-ated a furious debate among the public and academics. Were the authors right or wrong? Was their science correct or mistaken? Were the conclusions racist or realistic? A lot of oxygen was con-sumed in heated exchanges over these questions, and many peo-ple left those exchanges fairly confused.

However, viewing this issue through the lens of constructs actually makes it quite simple to understand. In *The Bell Curve*,

Herrnstein and Murray (1994, pp. 22–23) are very clear about their definition of intelligence, listing several assumptions, including:

1. There exists a general factor of cognitive ability that differs among human beings.
2. All standardized tests of academic aptitude or achievement measure this general factor to some degree, but IQ tests expressly designed for that purpose measure it most accurately.
3. IQ scores represent, to a first degree, whatever it is that people mean when they use the word *intelligent* or *smart* in ordinary language. IQ scores are stable, although not perfectly so, over much of a person's life.

Many scholars discussed in this book agree with these assumptions; others wouldn't agree with any of them. If you agree, then the next two of Herrnstein and Murray's assumptions are fairly logical. If you disagree, you probably have a big problem with them.

4. Properly administered IQ tests are not demonstrably biased against social, economic, ethnic, or racial groups.
5. Cognitive ability is substantially heritable—apparently no less than 40% and no more than 80%.

In the end, no matter what your view of intelligence and other cognitive phenomena, we can all agree on one thing: Constructs are critically important, and context matters to at least some degree.

NOTE

1. Specifically, we appreciate the willingness of several scholars to provide their time and input on a range of issues over the years: Camilla Benbow, Carolyn Callahan, Hudson Cattell

(grandson of James McKeen Cattell), Jack Cummings, J. P. Das, Douglas Detterman, Carol Dweck, Raymond Fancher, Donna Ford, Howard Gardner, Alan and Nadeen Kaufman, David Lubinski, Charles Murray, Jack Naglieri, Joe Renzulli, Dean Keith Simonton, and Bob Sternberg. In addition, Raymond Cattell and, especially, John Carroll and John Horn graciously (and extensively) provided their valuable, unique perspectives near the end of their lives.

Recommended Resources

The volume of material published on intelligence over the past 100 years is staggering, with a recent increase in the publication of both general overviews and research. To help make sense of this work, we recommend the following top 20 (roughly) of our favorite resources on human intelligence, with an emphasis on broad, accessible overviews.

Broad Overviews

Deary, I. J. (2001). *Intelligence: A very short introduction*. Oxford, UK: Oxford University Press.

> Definitely truth in advertising. This is a very short introduction, with an emphasis on classic views and research.

Fancher, R. E. (1985). *The intelligence men: Makers of the IQ controversy*. New York, NY: Norton.

> A classic historical overview, extremely engaging and written by an eminent historian of psychology. One of the most influential books on our approach to the topic.

Hunt, E. B. (2011). *Human intelligence*. Cambridge, UK: Cambridge University Press.

A well-written, highly accessible approach to some complex topics within the field.

Mackintosh, N. (2011). *IQ and human intelligence* (2nd ed.). Oxford, UK: Oxford University Press.

Yes, it's a textbook, but it's a very good textbook.

Neisser, U., Boodoo, G., Bouchard, T. J. Jr., Boykin, A. W., Brody, N., Ceci, S. J., … Urbina, S. (1996). Intelligence: Knowns and unknowns. *American Psychologist, 51*(2), 77–101.

Nisbett, R. E., Aronson, J., Blair, C., Dickens, W., Flynn, J., Halpern, D. F., & Turkheimer, E. (2012). Intelligence: New findings and theoretical developments. *American Psychologist,* doi: 10.1037/a0026699

We consider these two reviews to be companion pieces. Taken together, they provide a solid review of psychological research on intelligence over the past generation. Each article is written by an all-star team of scholars.

High-Quality Resources

These are not books you will curl up with on the couch with a glass of wine on a cold winter's night, but they are first-class, highly comprehensive resources.

Sternberg, R. J. (Ed.). (1994). *Encyclopedia of human intelligence*. New York, NY: Macmillan.

Sternberg, R. J. (Ed.). (2004). *International handbook of intelligence*. Cambridge, UK: Cambridge University Press.

Sternberg, R. J., & Kaufman, S. B. (Eds.). (2011). *The Cambridge handbook of intelligence*. Cambridge, UK: Cambridge University Press.

Wilhelm, O., & Engle, R. W. (Eds.). (2005). *Handbook of understanding and measuring intelligence*. London, UK: Sage.

Electronic Resources

Esping, A., & Plucker, J. A. (2013). Intelligence. In Dana S. Dunn (Ed.), *Oxford bibliographies: Psychology*. New York, NY: Oxford University Press. Retrieved from http://www.oxfordbibliographies.com/ view/document/obo-9780199828340/obo-9780199828340- 0092.xml?rskey=kNhrFK&result=23&q=]

Kaufman, S. B. (2011). Intelligence. In Luanna H. Meyer (Ed.), *Oxford bibliographies: Education*. New York, NY: Oxford University Press. Retrieved from http://www.oxfordbibliographiesonline.com/ view/document/obo-9780199756810/obo-9780199756810-0021 .xml

These two online bibliographies provide numerous detailed listings and descriptions of available resources, from both educational and psychological perspectives.

Plucker, J. A., & Esping, A. (Eds.). (2013). *Human intelligence: Historical influences, current controversies, teaching resources*. Retrieved from http://www.intelltheory.com

This site was created in 1998.

Overviews of Specific Topics

Ceci, S. J., & Williams, W. W. (2000). *The nature-nurture debate: The essential readings*. Oxford: Wiley-Blackwell, UK.

A comprehensive edited volume on the development of intelligence.

Johnson, W., Penke, L., & Spinath, F. M. (2011). Heritability in the era of molecular genetics: Some thoughts for understanding genetic influences on behavioral traits. *European Journal of Personality, 25*, 254–266.

An interesting analysis of the importance of behavior genetics research—and its limitations.

Kaufman, A. S. (2009). *IQ testing 101.* New York, NY: Springer Publishing Company.

> The title says it all, a book written by one of the giants of the field.

Plucker, J. A., & Callahan, C. M. (Eds.). (2008). *Critical issues and practices in gifted education: What the research says.* Waco, TX: Prufrock Press.

> This edited book summarizes research on 50 aspects of giftedness and gifted education.

Sternberg, R. J., & Davidson, J. E. (Eds.). (2005). *Conceptions of giftedness* (2nd ed.). New York, NY: Cambridge University Press.

> Both this volume and the earlier edition contain a "who's who" of the people working with theories of giftedness and talent.

Sternberg, R. J., & Grigorenko, E. L. (Eds.). (1997). *Intelligence, heredity and environment.* Cambridge, UK: Cambridge University Press.

> Another solid review of behavior genetics research as applied to the study of intelligence.

Subotnik, R. F., Olszewski-Kubilius, P., & Worrell, F. C. (2011). Rethinking giftedness and gifted education: A proposed direction forward based on psychological science. *Psychological Science in the Public Interest, 12*(1), 3–54.

> A seminal paper by three leading scholars that reviews psychological research on giftedness and proposes a new approach to developing intellectual talent.

Additional Works

Intelligence (http://www.journals.elsevier.com/intelligence)

> The major journal devoted solely to the study of intelligence. This bimonthly journal does not shy away from controversial topics, making it a must-read for people interested in a wide range of perspectives on the topic.

References

Achter, J. A., Benbow, C. P., & Lubinski, D. (1997). Rethinking multi-potentiality among the intellectually gifted: A critical review and recommendations. *Gifted Child Quarterly, 41*, 5–15.

Alivisatos, P. A., Chun, M., Church, G. M., Greenspan, R. J., Roukes, M. L., & Yuste, R. (2012). The Brain Activity Map Project and the challenge of functional connectomics. *Neuron, 74*, 970–974.

Almeida, L. S., Prieto, M. D., Ferreira, A. I., Bermejo, M. R., Ferrando, M., & Ferrándiz, C. (2010). Intelligence assessment: Gardner multiple intelligence theory as an alternative. *Learning and Individual Differences, 20*, 225–230.

Amabile, T. M. (1996). *Creativity in context: Update to "The social psychology of creativity."* Boulder, CO: Westview Press.

American Psychiatric Association. (2013). *Diagnostic and statistical manual of mental disorders: DSM-5.* Washington, DC: Author.

American Psychological Association. (2002). *Ethical principles of psychologists and code of conduct.* Retrieved March 24, 2006, from http://www.apa.org/ethics/code2002.html

Atkins v. Virginia, 536 U.S. 304 (2002).

Atlantic Monthly (1870, June). Reviews and literary notices, pp. 753–756.

Baltes, M. M., & Carstensen, L. L. (1996). The process of successful ageing. *Ageing and Society, 16*, 397–422.

Barab, S. A., & Plucker, J. A. (2002). Smart people or smart contexts? Talent development in an age of situated approaches to learning and thinking. *Educational Psychologist, 37*, 165–182.

Bar-On, R. (1997). *The Emotional Intelligence inventory (EQ-i): Technical manual.* Toronto, Canada: Multi-Health Systems.

Bar-On, R. (2000). Emotional and social intelligence: Insights from the Emotional Quotient inventory. In R. Bar-On & J. D. A. Parker (Eds.), *The handbook of emotional intelligence: Theory, development, assessment, and application at home, school, and in the workplace* (pp. 363–388). San Francisco, CA: Jossey-Bass.

Bar-On, R. (2005). The impact of emotional intelligence on subjective well-being. *Perspectives in Education, 23*(2), 1–22.

Bar-On, R., Handley, R., & Fund, S. (2005). The impact of emotional intelligence on performance. In V. Druskat, F. Sala, & G. Mount (Eds.), *Linking emotional intelligence and performance at work: Current research evidence* (pp. 3–20). Mahwah, NJ: Lawrence Erlbaum Associates.

Barron, F. (1969). *Creative person and creative process.* New York, NY: Holt, Rinehart, & Winston.

Beaty, R. E., & Silvia, P. J. (2012). Why do ideas get more creative across time? An executive interpretation of the serial order effect in divergent thinking tasks. *Psychology of Aesthetics, Creativity, and the Arts, 6*, 309–319.

Beaujean, A., & Osterlind, S. J. (2008). Using item response theory to assess the Flynn effect in the National Longitudinal Study of Youth 79 Children and Young Adults data. *Intelligence, 36*, 455–463.

Berg, C. A., & Sternberg, R. J. (1985). A triarchic theory of intellectual development during adulthood. *Developmental Review, 5*, 334–370.

Bickley, P. G., Keith, T. Z., & Wolfle, L. M. (1995). The three-stratum theory of cognitive abilities: Test of the structure of intelligence across the life span. *Intelligence, 20*, 309–328.

Binet, A., & Simon, T. (1905). Methodés nouvelles pour le diagnostic du niveau intellectual des anormaux. *L'Année Psychologique, 11*, 191–244.

Binet, A., & Simon, T. (1908). The development of intelligence in the child. *L'Année Psychologique, 14*, 1–90.

Binet, A., & Simon, T. (1916/1973). *The development of intelligence in children.* Baltimore, MD: Williams & Wilkins. (Reprinted 1973, New York, NY: Arno Press)

Black, E. (2003). *War against the weak: Eugenics and America's campaign to create a master race.* New York, NY: Four Walls Eight Windows.

Blair, C., & Raver, C. C. (2012). Individual development and evolution: Experiential canalization of self-regulation. *Developmental Psychology, 48*, 647–657. doi: 10.1037/a0026472

Bronfenbrenner, U., & Ceci, S. J. (1994). Nature-nurture reconceptualized in developmental perspective: A bioecological model. *Psychological Review, 101*, 568–586. doi: 10.1037/0033-295X.101.4.568

Burt, C. (1909). Experimental tests of general intelligence. *British Journal of Psychology, 3*(1–2), 94–177.

Burt, C. (1957). *The causes and treatments of backwardness* (4th ed.). London, UK: University of London Press.

Burt, C. (1969). Intelligence and heredity: some common misconceptions. *The Irish Journal of Education, 3*(2), 75–94.

Burt, C. L. (1966). The genetic determination of differences in intelligence: A study of monozygotic twins reared together and apart. *British Journal of Psychology, 57*, 137–153.

Callahan, C. M., Hunsaker, S. L., Adams, C. M., Moore, S. D., & Bland, L. C. (1995). *Instruments used in the identification of gifted and talented students* (Report No. RM-95130). Charlottesville, VA: National Research Center on the Gifted and Talented.

Carroll, J. B. (1993). *Human cognitive abilities: A survey of factor-analytical studies.* New York, NY: Cambridge University Press.

Carroll, J. B. (1995). Reflections on Stephen Jay Gould's "The Mismeasure of Man" (1981): A retrospective review. *Intelligence, 21*, 121–134.

Carroll, J. B. (1997). The three-stratum theory of cognitive abilities. In D. P. Flanagan, J. L. Genshaft, & P. L. Harrison (Eds.), *Contemporary intellectual assessment: Theories, tests, and issues* (pp. 122–130). New York, NY: Guilford Press.

Castejon, J. L., Perez, A. M., & Gilar, R. (2010). Confirmatory factor analysis of Project Spectrum activities: A second-order *g* factor or multiple intelligences? *Intelligence, 38*, 481–496.

Cattell, R. B. (1941). Some theoretical issues in adult intelligence testing. *Psychological Bulletin, 38*(592), 10.

Cattell, R. B. (1963). Theory of fluid and crystallized intelligence: A critical experiment. *Journal of Educational Psychology, 54*, 1–22.

Cattell, R. B. (1967). The theory of fluid and crystallized general intelligence checked at the 5–6 year-old level. *British Journal of Educational Psychology, 37*, 209–224.

Cattell, R. B. (1971). *Abilities: Their structure, growth, and action.* Boston, MA: Houghton Mifflin.

Cattell, R. B. (1987). *Intelligence: Its structure, growth, and action.* New York, NY: Elsevier.

Ceci, S. J., & Kanaya, T. (2010). "Apples and oranges are both round": Furthering the discussion on the Flynn effect. *Journal of Psychoeducational Assessment, 28,* 469–473.

Cherniss, C. (2010). Emotional intelligence: Toward clarification of a concept. *Industrial and Organizational Psychology, 3,* 110–126.

Cherniss, C., Extein, M., Goleman, D., & Weissberg, R. P. (2006). Emotional intelligence: What does the research really indicate? *Educational Psychologist, 41,* 239–245.

Churchill, W. (1944). *Onwards to victory.* London, UK: Cassell.

Cianciolo, A. T., & Sternberg, R. J. (2004). *Intelligence: A brief history.* Malden, MA: Blackwell.

Ciarrochi, J. V., Chan, A. Y., & Caputi, P. (2000). A critical evaluation of the emotional intelligence construct. *Personality and Individual Differences, 28,* 539–561.

Cole, J. C., & Randall, M. K. (2003). Comparing the cognitive ability models of Spearman, Horn and Cattell, and Carroll. *Journal of Psychoeducational Assessment, 21,* 160–179. doi: 10.1177/073428290302100204

Coleman, L. J., & Cross, T. L. (2001). Being gifted in school: An introduction to education, guidance, and teaching: Book review. *Gifted Child Quarterly, 45,* 65–67.

Colom, R., Lluis-Font, J. M., & Andres-Pueyo, A. (2005). The generational intelligence gains are caused by decreasing variance in the lower half of the distribution: Supporting evidence for the nutrition hypothesis. *Intelligence, 33,* 83–91.

D'Amico, A., Cardaci, M., Di Nuovo, S., & Naglieri, J. A. (2012). Differences in achievement not in intelligence in the north and south of Italy: Comments on Lynn (2010a, 2010b). *Learning and Individual Differences, 22,* 128–132.

Darwin, C. (1985). *The origin of species by means of natural selection; or, the preservation of favoured races in the struggle for life.* New York, NY: Penguin. (Original work published 1859)

Das, J. P. (2002). A better look at intelligence. *Current Directions in Psychological Science, 11,* 28–33.

Das, J. P., Kirby, J. R., & Jarman, R. F. (1975). Simultaneous and successive syntheses: An alternative model for cognitive abilities. *Psychological Bulletin, 82,* 87–103.

Das, J. P., Naglieri, J. A., & Kirby, J. R. (1994). *Assessment of cognitive processes: The PASS theory of intelligence.* Boston, MA: Allyn & Bacon.

Deary, I. J., Penke, L., & Johnson, W. (2010). The neuroscience of human intelligence differences. *Nature Reviews: Neuroscience, 11,* 201–211.

Deary, I. J., Whalley, L. J., & Starr, J. M. (2009). *A lifetime of intelligence: Follow-up studies of the Scottish Mental Surveys of 1932 and 1947.* Washington, DC: American Psychological Association.

Decker, J. R., Eckes, S. E., & Plucker, J. (2010). Charter schools designed for gifted and talented students: Legal and policy issues and considerations. *Education Law Reporter, 259*(1), 1–18.

Deiner, C. I., & Dweck, C. S. (1978). An analysis of learned helplessness: Continuous changes in performance, strategy and achievement cognitions following failure. *Journal of Personality and Social Psychology, 36,* 451–462.

Deiner, C. I., & Dweck, C. S. (1980). An analysis of learned helplessness: (II) The processing of success. *Journal of Personality and Social Psychology, 39,* 940–952.

Delisle, J. R., & Renzulli, J. S. (1982). The revolving door identification and programming model: Correlates of creative production. *Gifted Child Quarterly, 26,* 89–95.

Devlin, B., Fienberg, S. E., Resnick, D. P., & Roeder, K. (Eds.). (1997). *Intelligence, genes, and success: Scientists respond to* The Bell Curve. New York, NY: Springer-Verlag.

Diamond, J. M. (1999). *Guns, germs, and steel: The fates of human societies.* New York, NY: W. W. Norton.

Dickens, W. T., & Flynn, J. R. (2001). Heritability estimates versus large environmental effects: The IQ paradox resolved. *Psychological Bulletin, 108,* 346–369.

Dweck, C. S. (1975). The role of expectations and attributions in the alleviation of learned helplessness. *Journal of Personality and Social Psychology, 31,* 674–685.

Dweck, C. S. (1999). *Self-theories: Their role in motivation, personality and development*. Philadelphia, PA: Psychology Press.

Dweck, C. S. (2007). *Mindset: The new psychology of success*. New York, NY: Ballantine.

Eckes, S. E., & Plucker, J. A. (2005). Charter schools and gifted education: Legal obligations. *Journal of Law and Education, 34*, 421–436.

Edwards, A. J. (1994). Wechsler, David (1896–1981). In R. J. Sternberg (Ed.), *Encyclopedia of intelligence* (Vol. 1, pp. 1134–1136). New York, NY: Macmillan.

Ericsson, K. A., & Kintsch, W. (1995). Long-term working memory. *Psychological Review, 102*, 211–245.

Eysenck, H. J. (1979). *The structure and measurement of intelligence*. New York, NY: Springer-Verlag.

Fancher, R. E. (1983). Biographical origins of Francis Galton's psychology. *Isis, 74*, 227–233.

Fancher, R. E. (1985). *The intelligence men: Makers of the IQ controversy*. New York, NY: W. W. Norton.

Fancher, R. E. (1998). Biography and psychodynamic theory: Some lessons from the life of Francis Galton. *History of Psychology, 1*, 99–115.

Feldhusen, J. F. (1998). A conception of talent and talent development. In R. C. Friedman & K. B. Rogers (Eds.), *Talent in context: Historical and social perspectives on giftedness* (pp. 193–209). Washington, DC: American Psychological Association.

Fletcher, J. M., Stuebing, K. K., & Hughes, L. C. (2010). IQ scores should be corrected for the Flynn effect in high-stakes decisions. *Journal of Psychoeducational Assessment, 28*, 441–447.

Flynn, J. R. (1984). The mean IQ of Americans: Massive gains 1932 to 1978. *Psychological Bulletin, 95*, 29–51.

Flynn, J. R. (1987). Massive IQ gains in 14 nations: What IQ tests really measure. *Psychological Bulletin, 101*, 171–191.

Flynn, J. R. (1998). IQ gains over time: Toward finding the causes. In U. Neisser (Ed.), *The rising curve: Long-term gains in IQ and related measures* (pp. 25–66). Washington, DC: American Psychological Association.

Flynn, J. R. (1999). Searching for justice: The discovery of IQ gains over time. *American Psychologist, 54*, 5–20.

Flynn, J. R. (2006). Tethering the elephant: Capital cases, IQ, and the Flynn Effect. *Psychology, Public Policy, and Law, 12,* 170–189.

Flynn, J. R. (2007). *What is intelligence?* New York, NY: Cambridge University Press.

Flynn, J. R. (2009). *What is intelligence?* (Expanded ed.). New York, NY: Cambridge University Press.

Flynn, J. R. (2010). Problems with IQ gains: The huge vocabulary gap. *Journal of Psychoeducational Assessment, 28,* 412–433.

Flynn, J. R., & Weiss, L. G. (2007). American IQ gains from 1932 to 2002: The WISC subtests and educational progress. *International Journal of Testing, 7,* 209–224.

Forrest, D. W. (1974). *Francis Galton: The life and work of a Victorian genius.* London, UK: Elek.

Frederickson, N., Petrides, K. V., & Simmonds, E. (2012). Trait emotional intelligence as a predictor of socioemotional outcomes in early adolescence. *Personality and Individual Differences, 52,* 323–328.

Fuchs-Beauchamp, K. D., Karnes, M. B., & Johnson, L. J. (1993). Creativity and intelligence in preschoolers. *Gifted Child Quarterly, 37,* 113–117.

Gagné, F. (1993). Constructs and models pertaining to exceptional human abilities. In K. A. Heller, F. J. Mönks, & A. H. Passow (Eds.), *International handbook of research and development of giftedness and talent* (pp. 69–87). New York, NY: Pergamon Press.

Gagné, F. (1998). The prevalence of gifted, talented, and multitalented individuals: Estimates from peer and teacher nominations. In R. C. Friedman & K. B. Rogers (Eds.), *Talent in context: Historical and social perspectives on giftedness* (pp. 101–126). Washington, DC: American Psychological Association.

Gagné, F. (2000). Understanding the complex choreography of talent development through DMGT-based analysis. In K. A. Heller, F. J. Mönks, R. J. Sternberg, & R. F. Subotnik (Eds.), *International handbook of giftedness and talent* (2nd ed., pp. 67–80). New York, NY: Pergamon.

Gagné, F. (2005). From gifts to talents: The DMGT as a developmental model. In R. J. Sternberg & J. E. Davidson (Eds.), *Conceptions of giftedness* (2nd ed., pp. 98–119). New York, NY: Cambridge University Press.

Galton, E. (1840, October 23). (Letter to Francis Galton). Galton Archives File 105.

Galton, F. (1851, December 15). Mr. Galton's expedition in southern Africa. *The Times*, 5f.

Galton, F. (1853a). *Tropical South Africa*. London, UK: John Murray.

Galton, F. (1853b). Remarks on presentation of RGS gold medal. *Journal of the Royal Geographical Society, 23*, lviii–lxi.

Galton, F. (1861a). Meteorological charts. *Philosophical Magazine, 22*, 34–35.

Galton, F. (1861b). Zanzibar. *Mission Field, 6*, 121–130.

Galton, F. (1865). Hereditary talent and character. *Macmillan's Magazine, 12*, 157–166, 318–327.

Galton, F. (1869). *Hereditary genius: An inquiry into its laws and consequences*. London, UK: Macmillan.

Galton, F. (1873). Hereditary improvement. *Frasier's Magazine, 7*, 116–130.

Galton, F. (1874). *English men of science: Their nature and nurture*. London, UK: Macmillan.

Galton, F. (1875). The history of twins, as a criterion of the relative powers of nature and nurture. *Frasier's Magazine, 12*, 566–576.

Galton, F. (1883). *Inquiries into human faculty and its development*. London, UK: Macmillan.

Galton, F. (1884). *Hereditary genius*. New York, NY: D. Appleton.

Galton, F. (1885a). On the anthropometric laboratory at the late International Health Exhibition. *Journal of the Anthropological Institute, 14*, 205–218.

Galton, F. (1885b). Some results of the anthropometric laboratory. *Journal of the Anthropological Institute, 14*, 275–287.

Galton, F. (1892). *Hereditary genius: An inquiry into its laws and consequences* (2nd ed.). London: Macmillan.

Galton, F. (1894). *Natural inheritance* (5th ed.). New York, NY: Macmillan.

Gardner, H. (1983). *Frames of mind: The theory of multiple intelligences*. New York, NY: Basic Books.

Gardner, H. (1993). *Creating minds: An anatomy of creativity seen through the lives of Freud, Einstein, Picasso, Stravinsky, Eliot, Graham, and Gandhi*. New York, NY: Basic Books.

Gardner, H. (1995). Reflections on multiple intelligences: Myths and messages. *Phi Delta Kappan, 77*, 200–209.

Gardner, H. (1999). *Intelligence reframed: Multiple intelligences for the 21st century.* New York, NY: Basic Books.

Gardner, H. (2006). *Multiple intelligences: New horizons in theory and practice.* New York, NY: Basic Books.

Getzels, J. W., & Jackson, P. W. (1962). *Creativity and intelligence: Explorations with gifted students.* New York, NY: Wiley.

Goddard, H. H. (1908a). The Binet and Simon tests of intellectual capacity. *Training School Bulletin, 5*, 3–9.

Goddard, H. H. (1908b). The grading of backward children. *Training School Bulletin, 5*, 12–14.

Goddard, H. H. (1910). Four hundred feeble-minded children classified by the Binet method. *Journal of Psycho-Asthenics, 15*, 17–30.

Goddard, H. H. (1912a). *The Kallikak family: A study in the heredity of feeble-mindedness.* New York, NY: Macmillan.

Goddard, H. H. (1912b). Feeble-mindedness and immigration. *Training School Bulletin, 9*, 91–94.

Goddard, H. H. (1914). *Feeble-mindedness: Its causes and consequences.* New York, NY: Macmillan.

Goddard, H. H. (1917). Mental tests and the immigrant. *Journal of Delinquency, 2*, 243–277.

Goddard, H. H. (1920). *Human efficiency and levels of intelligence.* Princeton, NJ: Princeton University Press.

Goddard, H. H. (1927). Who is a moron? *Scientific Monthly, 24*(1), 41–46.

Goddard, H. H. (1928). Feeble-mindedness: A question of definition. *Journal of Psycho-Asthenics, 33*, 219–227.

Gottfredson, L. S. (1997). Mainstream science on intelligence: An editorial with 52 signatories, history, and bibliography. *Intelligence, 24*, 13–23.

Gottfredson, L. S., et al. (1994, December 13). Mainstream science on intelligence. *Wall Street Journal.*

Gould, S. J. (1981). *The mismeasure of man.* New York, NY: W. W. Norton.

Grigorenko, E. L., Wenzel Geissler, P., Prince, R., Okatcha, F., Nokes, C., Kenny, D. A., . . . Sternberg, R. J. (2001). The organisation of Luo conceptions of intelligence: A study of implicit theories in a

Kenyan village. *International Journal of Behavioral Development, 25,* 367–378.

Gubbins, E. J. (1982). *Revolving door identification model: Characteristics of talent pool students.* Unpublished doctoral dissertation, The University of Connecticut, Storrs.

Guilford, J. P. (1950). Creativity. *American Psychologist, 5,* 444–544.

Guilford, J. P. (1967). *The nature of human intelligence.* New York, NY: McGraw-Hill.

Hagan, L. D., Drogin, E. Y., & Guilmette, T. J. (2010). IQ scores should not be adjusted for the Flynn effect in capital punishment cases. *Journal of Psychoeducational Assessment, 28,* 474–476.

Hall, K. M., Irwin, M. M., Bowman, K. A., Frankenberger, W., & Jewett, D. C. (2005). Illicit use of prescribed stimulant medication among college students. *Journal of American College Health, 53*(4), 167–174.

Hayes, J. R. (1989). Cognitive processes in creativity. In J. A. Glover, R. R. Ronning, & C. R. Reynolds (Eds.), *Handbook of creativity* (pp. 135–145). New York, NY: Plenum Press.

Henmon, V. A. C. (1969). Intelligence and its measurement. In L. E. Tyler (Ed.), *Intelligence: Some recurring issues. An enduring problem in psychology* (pp. 16–18). New York, NY: Van Nostrand Reinhold. (Original work published 1912)

Herrnstein, R. J., & Murray, C. A. (1994). *The bell curve: Intelligence and class structure in American life.* New York, NY: Free Press.

Hertzog, C., & Schaie, K. W. (1986). Stability and change in adult intelligence: I. Analysis of longitudinal covariance structures. *Psychology and Aging, 1,* 159–171.

Hollingworth, L. S. (1942). *Children above 180 IQ Stanford-Binet: Origin and development.* Yonkers-on-Hudson, NY: World Book.

Horn, J. L. (1967). Intelligence: Why it grows, why it declines. *Transaction,* 23–31.

Horn, J. L. (1970). Organization of data on life-span development of human abilities. In L. R. Goulet & P. B. Baltes (Eds.), *Life-span developmental psychology: Research and theory.* New York, NY: Academic Press.

Horn, J. L. (1976). Human abilities: A review of research and theory in the early 1970s. *Annual Review of Psychology, 27,* 437–485. doi: 10.1146/annurev.ps.27.020176.002253

Horn, J. L. (1998). A basis for research on age differences in cognitive abilities. In J. J. McArdle & R. Woodcock (Eds.), *Human cognitive abilities in theory and practice* (pp. 57–92). Mahwah, NJ: Erlbaum.

Horn, J. L., & Cattell, R. B. (1966a). Refinement and test of the theory of fluid and crystallized general intelligences. *Journal of Educational Psychology, 57,* 253–270.

Horn, J. L., & Cattell, R. B. (1966b). Age differences in primary mental ability factors. *Journal of Gerontology, 21,* 210–220.

Horn, J. L., & Cattell, R. B. (1967). Age differences in fluid and crystallized intelligence. *Acta Psychologica, 26,* 107–129.

Horn, J. L., & Donaldson, G. (1976). On the myth of intellectual decline in adulthood. *American Psychologist, 31,* 701–719. doi: 10.1037/0003-066X.31.10.701

Horn, J. L., Donaldson, G., & Engstrom, R. (1981). Apprehension, memory, and fluid intelligence decline in adulthood. *Research on Aging, 3,* 33–84. doi: 10.1177/016402758131002

Horn, J. L., & McArdle, J. J. (2007). In R. Cudeck & R. C. MacCallum (Eds.), *Factor analysis at 100: Historical developments and future directions* (pp. 205–248). Mahwah, NJ: Lawrence Erlbaum.

Horn, J. L., & Noll, J. (1997). Human cognitive capabilities: Gf-Gc theory. In D. P. Flanagan, J. L. Genshaft, & P. L Harrison (Eds.), *Beyond traditional intellectual assessment: Contemporary and emerging theories, tests, and issues* (pp. 53–91). New York, NY: Guilford Press.

Hunt, E. (2011). *Human intelligence.* New York, NY: Cambridge University Press.

Hunt, E. (2012). What makes nations intelligent? *Perspectives in Psychological Science, 7,* 284–306.

Hyatt, S. (1997). Shared history of shame: Sweden's four-decade policy of forced sterilization and the Eugenics Movement in the United States. *Indiana International & Comparative Law Review, 8,* 475.

Jauk, E., Benedek, M., Dunst, B., & Neubauer, A. C. (2013). The relationship between intelligence and creativity: New support for the threshold hypothesis by means of empirical breakpoint detection. *Intelligence, 41,* 212–221.

Jensen, A. R. (1979). *Bias in mental testing.* New York, NY: Free Press.

Jensen, A. R. (1980). *Bias in mental testing.* London, UK: Methuen.

Jensen, A. R. (1994). Spearman, Charles Edward. In R. J. Sternberg (Ed.), *Encyclopedia of intelligence* (Vol. 1, pp. 1007–1014). New York, NY: Macmillan.

Jensen, A. R. (1998). *The g factor: The science of mental ability.* Westport, CT: Praeger.

Johnsen, S. (1999). Renzulli's model: Needed research. *Journal for the Education of the Gifted, 23*, 102–116.

Joseph, D. L., & Newman, D. A. (2010). Emotional intelligence: An integrative meta-analysis and cascading model. *Journal of Applied Psychology, 95*, 54–78.

Kamin, L. J. (1974). *The science and politics of IQ.* Potomac, MD: Lawrence Erlbaum.

Kanaya, T., Scullin, M. H., & Ceci, S. J. (2003). The Flynn effect and U.S. policies: The impact of rising IQ scores on American society via mental retardation diagnoses. *American Psychologist, 58*, 1–13.

Karnes, F. A., & Bean, S. M. (Eds.). (2001). *Methods and materials for teaching the gifted.* Waco, TX: Prufrock Press.

Kaufman, A. S. (1990). *Assessing adolescent and adult intelligence.* Boston, MA: Allyn & Bacon.

Kaufman, A. S. (2009). *IQ testing 101.* New York, NY: Springer.

Kaufman, A. S. (2010). "In what way are apples and oranges alike?" A critique of Flynn's interpretation of the Flynn Effect. *Journal of Psychoeducational Assessment, 28*, 382–398.

Kaufman, A. S., & Kaufman, N. L. (1993). *Kaufman Adolescent and Adult Intelligence Test (KAIT).* Circle Pines, MN: American Guidance Service.

Kaufman, A. S., & Kaufman, N. L. (2004). *The Kaufman Assessment Battery for Children* (2nd ed.). Circle Pines, MN: American Guidance Service.

Kaufman, A. S., & Weiss, L. G. (2010). Guest editors' introduction to the special issue of *JPA* on the Flynn effect. *Journal of Psychoeducational Assessment, 28*, 379–381.

Kaufman, S. B., Reynolds, M. R., Liu, X., Kaufman, A. S., & McGrew, K. S. (2012). Are cognitive *g* and academic achievement *g* one and the same *g*? An exploration on the Woodcock–Johnson and Kaufman tests. *Intelligence, 40*, 123–138. doi: 10.1016/j.intell.2012.01.009

Keith, T. Z., & Reynolds, M. R. (2010). Cattell–Horn–Carroll abilities and cognitive tests: What we've learned from 20 years of research. *Psychology in the Schools, 47,* 635–650.

Kerr, B. & Erb, C. (1991). Career counseling with academically talented students: Effects of a value-based intervention. *Journal of Counseling Psychology, 38,* 309–314.

Keyes, D. (1966). *Flowers for Algernon.* New York, NY: Bantam.

Kim, K. H. (2005). Can only intelligent people be creative? *Journal of Secondary Gifted Education, 16,* 57–66.

Kitano, M. K. (1999). Bringing clarity to "This thing called giftedness": A response to Dr. Renzulli. *Journal for the Education of the Gifted, 23,* 87–101.

Kris, E. (1952). *Psychoanalytic exploration of art.* New York, NY: International Universities Press.

Kuhn, T. S. (1962/2012). *The structure of scientific revolutions* (4th ed.), Chicago, IL: University of Chicago Press.

Larson, G. (1994). Armed services vocational aptitude battery. In R. J. Sternberg (Ed.), *Encyclopedia of intelligence* (Vol. 1, pp. 121–124). New York, NY: Macmillan.

Legree, P. J., Pifer, M. E., & Grafton, F. C. (1996). Correlations among cognitive abilities are lower for high ability groups. *Intelligence, 23,* 54–57.

Lim, W., Plucker, J., & Im, K. (2002). We are more alike than we think we are: Implicit theories of intelligence with a Korean sample. *Intelligence, 20,* 185–208.

Lohman, D. F. (2005). Review of Naglieri and Ford (2003): Does the Naglieri Nonverbal Ability Test identify equal proportions of high-scoring White, Black, and Hispanic students? *Gifted Child Quarterly, 49,* 19–28.

Lohman, D. F., & Gambrell, J. L. (2012). Using nonverbal tests to help identify academically talented children. *Journal of Psychoeducational Assessment, 30,* 25–44.

Lubinski, D., & Benbow, C. P. (2006). Study of mathematically precocious youth after 35 years: Uncovering antecedents for the development of math-science expertise. *Perspectives on Psychological Science, 1,* 316–345.

Luria, A. R. (1973). *The working brain*. New York, NY: Basic Books.

Lynn, R., & Harvey, J. (2008). The decline of the world's IQ. *Intelligence, 36*, 112–120.

MacKinnon, D. W. (1965). Personality and the realization of creative potential. *American Psychologist, 20*, 273–281.

Mackintosh, N. J. (1995). *Cyril Burt: Fraud or framed?* New York, NY: Oxford University Press.

Mackintosh, N. J. (2011). *IQ and human intelligence* (2nd ed.). Oxford, NY: Oxford University Press.

Mandelman, S. D., & Grigorenko, E. L. (2011). Intelligence: Genes, environments, and their interactions. In R. J. Sternberg & S. B. Kaufman (Eds.), *The Cambridge handbook of intelligence* (pp. 85–106). New York, NY: Cambridge University Press.

Marland, S. (1972). *Education of the gifted and talented* (Report to the Congress of the United States by the U.S. Commissioner of Education). Washington, DC: U.S. Government Printing Office.

Matthews, G., Zeidner, M., & Roberts, R. D. (2012). *Emotional intelligence 101*. New York, NY: Springer Publishing Company.

Mayer, J. D., Caruso, D. R., & Salovey, P. (2000). Emotional intelligence meets traditional standards for an intelligence. *Intelligence, 27*, 267–298.

Mayer, J. D., & Salovey, P. (1997). What is emotional intelligence? In P. Salovey & D. Sluyter (Eds.), *Emotional development and emotional intelligence: Implications for educators* (pp. 3–31). New York, NY: Basic Books.

McArdle, J. J., Ferrer-Caja, E., Hamagami, F., & Woodcock, R. W. (2002). Comparative longitudinal structural analyses of the growth and decline of multiple intellectual abilities over the life span. *Developmental Psychology, 38*, 115–142. doi: 10.1037/0012-1649 .38.1.115

McArdle, J. J., Hamagami, F., Meredith, W., & Bradway, K. P. (2000). Modeling the dynamic hypotheses of *gf-gc* theory using longitudinal life-span data. *Learning and Individual Differences, 12*, 53–79.

McGrew, K. S. (1997). Analysis of the major intelligence batteries according to a proposed comprehensive *Gf-Gc* framework.

In D. P. Flanagan, J. L. Genshaft, & P. L. Harrison (Eds.), *Contemporary intellectual assessment: Theories, tests, and issues* (pp. 151–179). New York, NY: Guilford Press.

McGrew, K. S. (2010). The Flynn effect and its critics: Rusty linchpins and "Lookin' for *g* and *Gf* in some of the wrong places." *Journal of Psychoeducational Assessment, 28,* 448–468.

McGuire, F. (1994). Army alpha and beta tests of intelligence. In R. J. Sternberg (Ed.), *Encyclopedia of intelligence* (Vol. 1, pp. 125–129). New York, NY: Macmillan.

Meaney, M. J. (2001). Nature, nurture, and the disunity of knowledge. *Annals of the New York Academy of Sciences, 935,* 50–61.

Meeker, M. N. (1969). *The structure of intellect: Its interpretation and uses.* Columbus, OH: Merrill.

Mercer, J. R. (1973). *Labeling the mentally retarded.* Berkeley, CA: University of California Press.

Milgram, R. M., & Hong, E. (1999). Multipotential abilities and vocational interests in gifted adolescents: Fact or fiction? *International Journal of Psychology, 34,* 81–93.

Mönks, F. J., & Mason, E. J. (1993). Developmental theories and giftedness. In K. A. Heller, F. J. Mönks, & A. H. Passow (Eds.), *International handbook of research and development of giftedness and talent* (pp. 89–101). New York, NY: Pergamon Press.

Moon, S. M., Kelly, K. R., & Feldhusen, J. F. (1997). Specialized counseling services for gifted youth and their families: A needs assessment. *Gifted Child Quarterly, 41,* 16–25.

Naglieri, J. A., & Das, J. P. (1997). *Das-Naglieri Cognitive Assessment System.* Itasca, IL: Riverside Publishing.

Naglieri, J. A., & Ford, D. Y. (2003). Addressing underrepresentaion of gifted minority children using the Naglieri Nonverbal Ability Test (NNAT). *Gifted Child Quarterly, 47,* 155–160.

Naglieri, J. A., & Ford, D. Y. (2005). Increasing minority children's participation in gifted classes using the NNAT: A response to Lohman. *Gifted Child Quarterly, 49,* 29–36.

Naglieri, J. A., & Ford, D. Y. (in press). Myths propagated about the Naglieri Nonverbal Ability Test: A commentary of concerns and disagreements. *Gifted Child Quarterly.*

Naglieri, J. A., & Kaufman, J. C. (2001). Understanding intelligence, giftedness and creativity using the PASS theory. *Roeper Review, 23*, 151–164.

Naglieri, J. A., & Otero, T. M. (2011). Cognitive Assessment System: Redefining intelligence from a neuropsychological perspective. In A. S. Davis (Ed.), *Handbook of pediatric neuropsychology* (pp. 320–333). New York, NY: Springer Publishing Company.

Naglieri, J. A., Rojahn, J., & Matto, H. C. (2007). Hispanic and non-Hispanic children's perfomance on PASS cognitive processes and achievement. *Intelligence, 35*, 568–579.

National Human Genome Research Institute (NHGRI). (2003, April 14). *International consortium completes Human Genome Project.* http://www.genome.gov/11006929

Nisbett, R. E. (2009). *Intelligence and how to get it.* New York, NY: Norton.

Nisbett, R. E., Aronson, J., Blair, C., Dickens, W., Flynn, J., Halpern, D. F., & Turkheimer, E. (2012). Intelligence: New findings and theoretical developments. *American Psychologist, 67*, 130–159.

Office of Educational Research and Improvement. (1993). *National excellence: A case for developing America's talents.* Washington, DC: U.S. Department of Education.

Olszewski-Kubilius, P. (1999). A critique of Renzulli's theory into practice models for gifted learners. *Journal for the Education of the Gifted, 23*, 55–66.

Oxford English Dictionary. (2011, June). retard, v. OED Online. Retrieved August 3, 2011, from http://www.oed.com.ezproxy.tcu.edu/view/Entry/164180?rskey=IMXSVk&result=2&isAadvanced=false

Park, G., Lubinski, D., & Benbow, C. P. (2007). Contrasting intellectual patterns for creativity in the arts and sciences: Tracking intellectually precocious youth over 25 years. *Psychological Science, 18*, 948–952.

Park, G., Lubinski, D., & Benbow, C. P. (2008). Ability differences among people who have commensurate degrees matter for scientific creativity. *Psychological Science, 19*, 957–961.

Passow, A. H. (1979). A look around and a look ahead. In A. H. Passow (Ed.), *The gifted and talented: Their education and development, the 78th yearbook of the National Society for the Study of Education* (pp. 447–451). Chicago, IL: NSSE.

Passow, A. H., & Rudnitski, R. A. (1993). *State policies regarding education of the gifted as reflected in legislation and regulation* [Collaborative Research Study CRS93302]. Storrs, CT: National Research Center on the Gifted and Talented.

Petrides, K. V. (2011). Ability and trait emotional intelligence. In T. Chamorro-Premuzic, A. Furnham, & S. von Stumm (Eds.), *The Blackwell-Wiley handbook of individual differences* (pp. 656–678). New York, NY: Wiley.

Petrides, K. V., & Furnham, A. (2003). Trait emotional intelligence: Behavioural validation in two studies of emotion recognition and reactivity to mood induction. *European Journal of Personality, 17*, 39–57.

Pintner, R. (1969). Intelligence and its measurement. In L. E. Tyler (Ed.), *Intelligence: Some recurring issues. An enduring problem in psychology* (pp. 13–14). New York, NY: Van Nostrand Reinhold Company. (Original work published 1912)

Plato. (1985). *Meno* (R. W. Sharples, Trans.) Chicago, IL: Bolchazy-Carducci. (Original work published ca. 390 BCE)

Plucker, J. (2000). Flip sides of the same coin or marching to the beat of different drummers? A response to Pyryt. *Gifted Child Quarterly, 44*, 193–195.

Plucker, J. (2008). Gifted education. In C. J. Russo (Ed.), *Encyclopedia of education law* (pp. 380–382). Thousand Oaks, CA: Sage.

Plucker, J., & Barab, S. A. (2005). The importance of contexts in theories of giftedness: Learning to embrace the messy joys of subjectivity. In R. J. Sternberg & J. A. Davidson (Eds.), *Conceptions of giftedness* (2nd ed., pp. 201–216). New York, NY: Cambridge University Press.

Plucker, J., Burroughs, N., & Song, R. (2010). *Mind the (other) gap! The growing excellence gap in K–12 education.* Bloomington, IN: Center for Evaluation and Education Policy.

Plucker, J., & Callahan, C. M. (Eds.). (2008). *Critical issues and practices in gifted education: What the research says.* Waco, TX: Prufrock Press.

Plucker, J., & Callahan, C. M. (Eds.). (2013). *Critical issues and practices in gifted education: What the research says* (2nd ed.). Waco, TX: Prufrock Press.

Plucker, J., Callahan, C. M., & Tomchin, E. M. (1996). Wherefore art thou, multiple intelligences? Alternative assessments for identifying talent in ethnically diverse and economically disadvantaged students. *Gifted Child Quarterly, 40*, 81–92.

Plucker, J. A., Beghetto, R. A., & Dow, G. T. (2004). Why isn't creativity more important to educational psychologists? Potentials, pitfalls, and future directions in creativity research. *Educational Psychologist, 39*, 83–96.

Preckel, F., Holling, H., & Wiese, M. (2006). Relationship of intelligence and creativity in gifted and non-gifted students: An investigation of threshold theory. *Personality and Individual Differences, 40*, 159–170.

Proctor, R. (2001). What causes cancer? A political history of recent debates. In R. S. Singh, C. B. Krimbas, D. B. Paul, & J. Beatty (Eds.), *Thinking about evolution: Historical, philosophical and political perspectives* (pp. 569–582). New York, NY: Cambridge University Press.

Pyryt, M. C. (2000). Finding "g": Easy viewing through higher order factor analysis. *Gifted Child Quarterly, 44*, 190–192.

Ramos-Ford, V., & Gardner, H. (1997). Giftedness from a multiple intelligences perspective. In N. Colangelo & G. A. David (Eds.), *Handbook of gifted education* (2nd ed.). Boston, MA: Allyn & Bacon.

Raven, J. C. (1938). *Progressive matrices*. London: Lewis.

Raven, J. C. (2000). *Raven manual research supplement 3: Neuropsychological applications*. Oxford, UK: Oxford Psychologists Press.

Renzulli, J. S. (1973). *New directions in creativity*. New York, NY: Harper & Row.

Renzulli, J. S. (1978). What makes giftedness? Reexamining a definition. *Phi Delta Kappan, 60*, 180–184, 261.

Renzulli, J. S. (1999). Reflections, perceptions, and future directions. *Journal for the Education of the Gifted, 23*, 125–146.

Renzulli, J. S. (2005). The three-ring definition of giftedness: A developmental model for promoting creative productivity. In R. J. Sternberg & J. E. Davidson (Eds.), *Conceptions of giftedness* (2nd ed., pp. 246–280). New York, NY: Cambridge University Press.

Renzulli, J. S. (Ed.). (1984). *Technical report of research studies related to the Revolving Door Identification Model* (2nd ed.). Storrs, CT: University of Connecticut Bureau of Educational Research and Service.

Renzulli, J. S. (Ed.). (1988). *Technical report of research studies related to the Revolving Door Identification Model* (2nd ed., Vol. II). Storrs, CT: University of Connecticut Bureau of Educational Research and Service.

Renzulli, J. S., & D'Souza, S. (2013). Intelligences outside the normal curve: Co-cognitive factors that contribute to the creation of social capital and leadership skills in young people. In J. A. Plucker & C. M. Callahan (Eds.), *Critical issues and practices in gifted education: What the research says* (2nd ed.). Waco, TX: Prufrock Press.

Renzulli, J. S., & Reis, S. M. (1985). *The schoolwide enrichment model: A comprehensive plan for educational excellence.* Mansfield Center, CT: Creative Learning Press.

Renzulli, J. S., & Sytsma, R. E. (2008). Intelligences outside the normal curve: Co-cognitive traits that contribute to giftedness. In J. A. Plucker & C. M. Callahan (Eds.), *Critical issues and practices in gifted education: What the research says* (pp. 57–84). Waco, TX: Prufrock Press.

Reynolds, C. R., Niland, J., Wright, J. E., & Rosenn, M. (2010). Failure to apply the Flynn correction in death penalty litigation: Standard practice of today maybe, but certainly malpractice tomorrow. *Journal of Psychoeducational Assessment, 28,* 477–481.

Ridley, M. (2003). *Nature via nurture: Genes, experience, and what makes us human.* New York, NY: HarperCollins.

Robinson, N. M. (1997). The role of universities and colleges in educating gifted undergraduates. *Peabody Journal of Education, 72,* 217–236.

Robinson, N. M. (2005). In defense of a psychometric approach to the definition of academic giftedness: A conservative view from a die-hard liberal. In R. J. Sternberg & J. E. Davidson (Eds.), *Conceptions of giftedness* (2nd ed., pp. 280–294). New York, NY: Cambridge University Press.

Robinson, N. M., Zigler, E., & Gallagher, J. J. (2000). Two tails of the normal curve: Similarities and differences in the study of mental retardation and giftedness. *American Psychologist, 55,* 1413–1424.

Rodgers, J. L. (1998). A critique of the Flynn effect: Massive IQ gains, methodological artifacts, or both? *Intelligence, 26,* 337–356.

Rodgers, J. L., & Wanstrom, L. (2007). Identification of a Flynn effect in the NLSY: Moving from the center to the boundaries. *Intelligence, 35*, 187–196.

Rogers, A. C. (1910). The new classification (tentative) of the Feeble-Minded [Editorial]. *Journal of Psycho-Asthenics, 15*, 70.

Rosa's Law. (2010). Pub. L. No. 111–256, Stat 2781-3.

Rushton, J. P., & Jensen, A. R. (2005). Thirty years of research on race differences in cognitive ability. *Psychology, Public Policy, and Law, 11*, 235–294.

Rysiew, K. J., Shore, B. M., & Leeb, R. T. (1999). Multipotentiality, giftedness, and career choice: A review. *Journal of Counseling & Development, 77*, 423–430.

Schaie, K. W. (1994). The course of adult intellectual development. *American Psychologist, 49*, 304–313.

Schaie, K. W. (2005). *Developmental influences on adult intelligence: The Seattle Longitudinal Study.* Oxford: Oxford University Press.

Schalock, R., Borthwick-Duffy, S., Bradley, V., Buntinx, W., Couldter, D., Craig, E., . . . Yeager, M. (2010). *Intellectual disability: Definition, classification, and systems of support* (11th ed.). Washington, DC: American Association on Intellectual and Developmental Disabilities.

Schalock, R. L., Luckasson, R. A., & Shogren, K. A. (2007). Perspectives: The renaming of mental retardation: Understanding the change to the term intellectual disability. *Intellectual and Developmental Disabilities, 45*, 116–124.

Schoen, J. (2001). Between choice and coercion: Women and the politics of sterilization in North Carolina, 1929–1975. *Journal of Women's History, 13*, 132–156.

Shurkin, J. (1992). *Terman's kids: The groundbreaking study of how the gifted grow up.* Boston, MA: Little, Brown.

Silver, M. G. (2003). Eugenics and compulsory sterilization laws: Providing redress for the victims of a shameful era in United States history. *George Washington Legal Review, 72*, 862.

Silverman, L. K. (2012). *Giftedness 101.* New York, NY: Springer Publishing Company.

Simons, S. B., Caruana, D. A., Zhao, M., & Dudek, S. M. (2011). Caffeine-induced synaptic potentiation in hippocampal CA2 neurons. *Nature Neuroscience, 15*, 23–25.

Simonton, D. K. (1994). *Greatness: Who makes history and why.* New York, NY: Guilford Press.

Simonton, D. K. (2009). *Genius 101.* New York, NY: Springer Publishing Company.

Sligh, A. C., Conners, F. A., & Roskos-Ewoldsen, B. (2005). Relation of creativity to fluid and crystallized intelligence. *Journal of Creative Behavior, 39,* 123–136.

Snow, R. E. (1992). Aptitude theory: Yesterday, today, and tomorrow. *Educational Psychologist, 27,* 5–32.

Spearman, C. (1904). "General intelligence," objectively determined and measured. *American Journal of Psychology, 15,* 201–293.

Spearman, C. (1923). *The nature of "intelligence" and the principles of cognition* (2nd ed.). London, UK: Macmillan.

Spearman, C. (1930). Autobiography. In C. Murchison (Ed.), *A history of psychology in autobiography* (Vol. 1, pp. 199–333). Worcester, MA: Clark University Press.

Spearman, C., & Jones, L. W. (1950). *Human ability.* London, UK: Macmillan.

Staff, R. T., Murray, A. D., Ahearn, T. S., Mustafa, N., Fox, H. C., & Whalley, L. J. (2012). Childhood socioeconomic status and adult brain size: Childhood socioeconomic status influences adult hippocampal size. *Annals of Neurology, 71,* 653–660.

Stanley, J. C. (1980). On educating the gifted. *Educational Researcher, 9,* 8–12.

Stanley, J. C., & Benbow, C. P. (1981). Using the SAT to find intellectually talented seventh graders. *College Board Review, 122,* 2–7, 26–27.

Steen, R. G. (2009). *Human intelligence and medical illness: Assessing the Flynn effect.* New York, NY: Springer Publishing Company.

Sternberg, R. J. (1984). What should intelligence tests test? Implications of a triarchic theory of intelligence for intelligence testing. *Educational Researcher, 13,* 5–15.

Sternberg, R. J. (1988). *The triarchic mind: A new theory of human intelligence.* New York, NY: Viking.

Sternberg, R. J. (1996). *Successful intelligence: How practical and creative intelligence determine success in life.* New York, NY: Simon & Schuster.

Sternberg, R. J. (1999a). Intelligence. In M. A. Runco & S. R. Pritzker (Eds.), *Encyclopedia of creativity: Volume 2* (pp. 81–88). San Diego, CA: Academic Press.

Sternberg, R. J. (1999b). The theory of successful intelligence. *Review of General Psychology, 3,* 292–316.

Sternberg, R. J. (2010). The Flynn effect: So what? *Journal of Psychoeducational Assessment, 28*(5), 434–440.

Sternberg, R. J. (2011a). From intelligence to leadership: A brief intellectual autobiography. *Gifted Child Quarterly, 55,* 309–312. doi: 10.1177/0016986211421872

Sternberg, R. J. (2011b). The theory of successful intelligence. In R. J. Sternberg & S. B. Kaufman (Eds.), *The Cambridge handbook of intelligence* (pp. 504–527). New York, NY: Cambridge University Press.

Sternberg, R. J., & Davidson, J. E. (Eds.). (1986). *Conceptions of giftedness.* New York, NY: Cambridge University Press.

Sternberg, R. J., & Kaufman, S. B. (2012). Trends in intelligence research. *Intelligence, 40,* 235–236.

Sternberg, R. J., Lautrey, J., & Lubart, T. I. (2003). *Models of intelligence: International perspectives.* Washington, DC: American Psychological Association.

Sternberg, R. J., & Lubart, T. I. (1995). *Defying the crowd.* New York, NY: Free Press.

Sternberg, R. J., & O'Hara, L. A. (1999). Creativity and intelligence. In R. J. Sternberg (Ed.), *Handbook of creativity* (pp. 251–272). New York, NY: Cambridge University Press.

Stevens, S. S. (1946). On the theory of scales of measurement. *Science, 103*(2684), 677–680.

Subotnik, R. F., Olszewski-Kubilius, P., & Worrell, F. C. (2011). Rethinking giftedness and gifted education: A proposed direction forward based on psychological science. *Psychological Science in the Public Interest, 12,* 3–54.

Subotnik, R. F., Olszewski-Kubilius, P., & Worrell, F. C. (2012). A proposed direction forward for gifted education based on psychological science. *Gifted Child Quarterly, 56,* 176–188. doi: 10.1177/0016986212456079

Sundet, J. M., Barlaug, D. F., & Torjussen, T. M. (2004). The end of the Flynn effect? A study of secular trends in mean intelligence scores of Norwegian conscripts during half a century. *Intelligence, 32,* 349–362.

Taub, G. E., & McGrew, K. S. (2004). A confirmatory factor analysis of Cattell–Horn–Carroll theory and cross-age invariance of the Woodcock-Johnson Tests of Cognitive Abilities III. *School Psychology Quarterly, 19,* 72–87.

Teasdale, T. W., & Owen, D. R. (2005). A long-term rise and recent decline in intelligence test performance: The Flynn effect in reverse. *Personality and Individual Differences, 39,* 837–843.

Terman, L. M. (1921). Intelligence and its measurement: A symposium. *Journal of Educational Psychology, 12*(3), 127–133.

Thomson, G. (1939). *The factorial analysis of human ability.* London, UK: University of London Press.

Thorndike, R. L. (1977). Causation of Binet IQ decrements. *Journal of Educational Measurement, 14,* 197–202.

Thorndike, R. L. (1997). *Measurement and evaluation in psychology and education* (6th ed.). Upper Saddle River, NJ: Prentice Hall.

Thurstone, L. L. (1936). A new conception of intelligence. *Educational Record, 17,* 441–450.

Thurstone, L. L. (1938). *Primary mental abilities.* Chicago, IL: University of Chicago Press.

Thurstone, L. L. (1946). Theories of intelligence. *Scientific Monthly, 62,* 101–112.

Thurstone, L. L. (1952). L. L. Thurstone [autobiography]. In G. Lindzey (Ed.), *A history of psychology in autobiography* (Vol. VI, pp. 294–321). Englewood Cliffs, NJ: Prentice Hall.

Thurstone, L. L. (1973). *The nature of intelligence.* London, UK: Routledge. (Original work published 1924)

Tigner, R. B., & Tigner, S. S. (2000). Triarchic theories of intelligence: Aristotle and Sternberg. *History of Psychology, 3,* 168–176.

Tyler, L. E. (1969). *Intelligence: Some recurring issues: An enduring problem in psychology.* Oxford, UK: Van Nostrand Reinhold.

van de Vijver, F. J. R., Mylonas, K., Pavlopoulos, V., & Georgas, J. (2003). Methodology of combining the WISC-III data sets. In J. Georgas, L. G. Weiss, F. J. R. van de Vijver, & D. H. Saklofske (Eds.), *Culture and children's intelligence: Cross-cultural analysis of the WISC-III* (pp. 265–276). San Diego, CA: Academic Press.

Visser, B. A., Ashton, M. C., & Vernon, P. A. (2006). Beyond *g*: Putting multiple intelligences theory to the test. *Intelligence, 34,* 487–502.

Wai, J., & Putallaz, M. (2011). The Flynn effect puzzle: A 30-year examination from the right tail of the ability distribution provides some missing pieces. *Intelligence, 39,* 443–455.

Waterhouse, L. (2006). Multiple intelligences, the Mozart effect, and emotional intelligence: A critical review. *Educational Psychologist, 41,* 207–225.

Watson, J. B. (1930). *Behaviorism.* Chicago, IL: University of Chicago Press.

Wechsler, D. (1939). *The measurement of adult intelligence.* Baltimore, MD: Williams & Wilkins.

Wechsler, D. (1940). Non-intellective factors in general intelligence. *Psychological Bulletin, 37,* 444–445.

Wechsler, D. (1944). *The measurement of adult intelligence* (3rd ed.). Baltimore, MD: Williams & Wilkins.

Wechsler, D. (1949). *Manual for the Wechsler Intelligence Scale for Children (WISC).* New York, NY: Psychological Corporation.

Wechsler, D. (1955). *Manual for the Wechsler Adult Intelligence Scale.* San Antonio, TX: The Psychological Corporation.

Wechsler, D. (1974). *Manual for the Wechsler Intelligence Scale for Children–Revised (WISC-R).* New York, NY: Psychological Corporation.

Wechsler, D. (1991). *Manual for the Wechsler Intelligence Scale for Children–Third Edition (WISC-III).* San Antonio, TX: Psychological Corporation.

Willis, J. O., Dumont, R., & Kaufman, A. S. (2011). Factor-analytic models of intelligence. In R. J. Sternberg & S. B. Kaufman (Eds.), *The Cambridge handbook of intelligence* (pp. 39–57). New York, NY: Cambridge University Press.

Wissler, C. (1901). The correlation of mental and physical tests. *Psychological Review Monograph Supplements, 3*(6).

Worrell, F. C., Olszewski-Kubilius, P., & Subotnik, R. F. (2012). Important issues, some rhetoric, and a few straw men: A response to comments on "Rethinking giftedness and gifted education." *Gifted Child Quarterly, 56,* 224–231. doi: 10.1177/0016086212456080

Yamamoto, K. (1964a). A further analysis of the role of creative thinking in high-school achievement. *The Journal of Psychology, 58,* 277–283.

Yamamoto, K. (1964b). Threshold of intelligence in academic achievement of highly creative students. *The Journal of Experimental Education, 32,* 401–405.

Yang, Z., Zhu, J., Pinon, M., & Wilkins, C. (2006, August). *Comparison of the Bayley III and the Bayley II.* Paper presented at the annual meeting of the American Psychological Association, New Orleans, LA.

Yerkes, R. M., & Yerkes, A. W. (1929). *The great apes: A study of anthropoid life.* New Haven, CT: Yale University Press.

Zenderland, L. (1998). *Measuring minds: Henry Herbert Goddard and the origins of American intelligence testing.* Cambridge, UK: Cambridge University Press.

Zhou, X., & Zhu, J. (2007, August). *Peeking inside the "blackbox" of Flynn Effect: Evidence from three Wechsler instruments.* Paper presented at the 115th annual convention of the American Psychological Association, San Francisco, CA.

Zhou, X., Zhu, J., & Weiss, L. G. (2010). Peeking inside the "black box" of the Flynn effect: Evidence from three Wechsler instruments. *Journal of Psychoeducational Assessment, 28,* 399–411.

Index